NEIGHBOURS . . . DON'T YOU JUST LOVE THEM?

Neighbours . . .
Don't You Just Love Them?

HILARY COOK

KINGSWAY PUBLICATIONS
EASTBOURNE

First published 1992

Unless otherwise indicated, biblical quotations are from the
Good News Bible © American Bible Society 1976.
AV = Authorised Version. Crown Copyright.
NIV = New International Version © 1973,
1978, 1984 by the International Bible Society.

Front cover illustration by Taffy Davies

ISBN: 0 86065 994 1

Printed in Great Britain for
KINGSWAY PUBLICATIONS LTD
1 St Anne's Road, Eastbourne, E Sussex BN21 3UN by
Richard Clay Ltd, Bungay, Suffolk
Typeset by J&L Composition Ltd, Filey, North Yorkshire

In Matthew 19:19 Jesus tells the young ruler—and us—to love our neighbour as we love ourselves.

And in Luke 10:30–37 he tells the religious teacher—and us—through the good Samaritan story, who our neighbour is.

So here is a book of encouragement, written because of the hard fact that when Jesus tells us to love our neighbours he doesn't allow us to choose which ones.

(I'm very grateful, though, that he chose my 'neighbours' Jean and Mary to be my nothing-too-much-trouble good Samaritans for all the typing!)

Contents

*The five sets of discussion-group material, one at the end of each
section, are full enough to allow the reader to decide which subjects are
of most interest to his or her particular group, if time is short.*

Foreword

It was the close of a women's day conference in Sheffield several years ago, and I found myself working my way down a small line of people wanting questions answered, or prayer for personal needs. The last person I came to was warm, friendly, but to the point. After a few minutes of chat she pushed a paperback into my hand, saying modestly, 'I thought you might like a copy of my book.' It was, of course, Hilary Cook speaking, offering me a copy of *What Will the Neighbours Say?*, her first book for Kingsway. I thanked her and tucked it into my briefcase with barely a second glance.

Later, on the train journey back to London, I took it out for a closer look, and by the time the train chugged into St Pancras I was completely absorbed and had almost finished the book! It appealed to me enormously, and in the following months I often found myself recommending it to groups and individuals to encourage them to reach out to others in Jesus' name. It was not any weighty teaching in the book that gave it its power, I felt, but the inspiration of the living illustrations shared by its author, usually involving her own life. It simply showed that evangelism is accessible to us all, and this second book of Hilary's carries the same punch! It is full of human and humorous stories of divinely appointed encounters with others, many of which result in lives changed, hearts and bodies healed and human beings restored to fellowship with their heavenly Father.

It seems to me that there are two ways of looking at the task of world evangelism. One is the 'eagle's eye view' which looks down at the broad canvas and sees everything flowing together in a majestic cosmic design. The other is the 'snail's eye view' which sees the needs and opportunities close at hand, and which operates out of the safe haven of 'home' wherever it goes, since it carries its home on its back! This may seem a slow or insignificant approach to the task, but no one who has been out and about early on a spring morning and seen the gleaming trails all over paths and walls would doubt that snails make an amazing amount of silent, steady, shining progress! The same is true of Hilary's approach to the great task of winning the world. I see no reason why these shining trails of snail-like splendour should not criss-cross the earth if we all follow her example and reach out to the people around us in Jesus' name.

Faith Forster
Ichthus Christian Fellowship

PROLOGUE

A False Start, for Starters!

Saturday morning dawns bright and clear, but I don't. My mind is muzzy, my feelings are flat and my body is quite devoid of all 'get up and go'. 'And, to make matters worse,' I moan to David, my already-dressed other half, 'I've far more to fit into this particular Saturday than seems humanly possible.'

'Right, Hilary,' he encourages me, well-motivated already, 'start rationalising.'

He must be joking! And he probably is, but he's pretending he's not. 'What can you eliminate or postpone?' he continues. 'Where can you delegate? What's the order of importance? Importance, not urgency, mind. And then rearrange everything for streamlining the synchronisation.'

Well, as you can tell, David's been on some pretty powerful personnel-management courses, and knows how to programme my muddled grey-cell computer with plenty of creative ideas. It's just working them out that's too much effort! So as he goes downstairs for his early morning cuppa, he leaves me still totally lacking in initiative to get out of bed. . . .

One trick I've learned over the years, though, whenever I've been absolutely stuck, is to try prayer. Having a personal hotline to my heavenly Father is a privilege I don't deserve. But, like millions of Christians around this planet, I've found he's always ready to answer—even if sometimes I'd rather not hear what he's saying.

When that happens it's a sure sign that I'm trying to run my own life instead of letting him do it. And I need to abdicate double-quick if I'm to keep on hearing his voice. When *I'm* sitting on the throne of my life, instead of the King of kings, I'm no longer able to communicate with him like a King's kid should. But he's ready to communicate with me again, the minute that throne is empty for him. It reminds me of the little boy singing as he came out of Sunday School the lovely old hymn 'God is still on the throne'. Only he'd misheard, and his alternative version was even better—God is still on the phone!

And so as I lie in bed on this uninspiring Saturday morning, I dial God's emergency phone number. Have you ever tried it? It's not 999—it's 333! Jeremiah 33:3 actually. 'Call to me, and I will answer you; I will tell you wonderful and marvellous things that you know nothing about.'

'Honestly, Father,' I start, 'I know I'm meant to be a King's kid, but I'm feeling more like a maid-of-all-work! All right. You've told us to "love our neighbour as ourselves"—whoever it is. But do we have to know so many neighbours in need? I'm really feeling it isn't safe for me to get out of bed nowadays! We just can't afford the time to know any more neighbours. But there are lots more needy people all around us. . . .' The heavens are still seeming like lead to me though, so I pull the blankets tighter around me and try again.

'You know I'm happy, Lord—most of the time, anyway, caring about the suicidal teenagers and desperate mums you seem to specialise in sending us. And the smelly old tramps, and the lonely neglected old ladies, plus the people who seem to have everything this world can offer, except knowing you. Not to mention all the perfectly ordinary, usually contented friends you surround us with, too. But there *is* a limit to how many people we can relate to at once—especially when we're working wives with five children. And did you take into account the sheer volume of need when you told us to love our neighbours? I wouldn't mind if only we could love them on a rota, one at a time. And, most of all, if you'd let us *choose* our neighbours too.'

I've hardly drawn breath in this one-sided conversation, interrupted only by David happily practising the hymns for tomorrow's service, on our old piano. And I know very well that it's long past the time for me to get up. Even impossible days—and especially those—need to begin for me with what used to be called (when I was converted as a teenager) a 'quiet time'. The only way it can be a quiet time in our house, though, is when I get up an hour before everyone else.

David's prayer and Bible-reading fits well into his lunch-break, but my lunch-break is often the busiest part of the day. It's crammed with left-over jobs I haven't been able to fit into the morning timetable, vying for my time with phone calls, often extra people to feed, and the famous Cook emergency taxi-service. So my quiet time usually has to happen before the house awakes, interrupted only by the dawn chorus.

But as I lie disconsolately in bed this miserable morning, even the dawn chorus fails to move me. 'Well, a quiet time isn't much help, Lord,' I'm arguing, 'when you tell us to love our neighbours, and then send us far too many of them, and. . . .'

Suddenly the early morning milk-float arrives, and then the world drowns me out—with an ambulance racing down the road, its siren blaring for a second as it passes our congested part of the road. It makes me jump, and the surge of accompanying adrenalin stirs my mind into action. I'm reminded of how stupid it is to break a good habit pattern acquired over many struggling months—the habit of meeting the one Person who really matters, at the time when I can hear him best. Missing that appointment even once always means it's harder to keep the next morning.

So I'm soon downstairs with David, belatedly opening the Bible at 1 Peter 5:7 and starting to see everything from a new perspective. 'Casting all your care upon him,' it says. 'OK, Lord,' I answer, 'I'm doing just that. Instead of grumbling about numbers, I'm just going to trust you about any new neighbours you care to send, knowing you'll show me who to say "no" to. And "no" or "yes", I'll just concentrate on the loving them bit.' (Sometimes it's harder, and more loving, to say 'no' to people who should be turning elsewhere than to say 'yes'.) 'But please, Lord, could you give us a bit of a breather while we concentrate on the ones you've given us already?'

However, as I've said already, the King of kings has to be on the throne of our lives. So later on that very same Saturday, he forcibly reminds me of that fact. He does it by answering my prayer in a most breath-taking way, but not at all in the way I'd wanted. It all begins when I arrive home from work. On Saturday mornings David enjoys (most of the time) a stint of looking after the children, while I practise dentistry. ('When will you be able to do it properly?' asks six-year-old Stephanie, newly aware of the rigours of needing to practise the piano!)

On this particular Saturday, one of the many items on the agenda, between shopping, taking children to a party, doing a local radio interview, and so on, is to give two elderly friends a treat. Nora and Molly live a distance from each other, but I'm taking them both to Open House—our local Christian outreach café-cum-bookshop—for a dainty afternoon tea. I can't join them because that half-hour is the only slot I've got for racing round the supermarket with eleven-year-old John and little sister Stephanie, amassing the weekend's needs. As we leave Open House a man in a pink fluffy duck suit walks up to it, and us, with a collecting tin for handicapped children. Our adopted son John happens, of course, to be handicapped by a faulty heart, but I haven't got any change so, sadly, that's that.

Except it isn't. Because as we arrive back half an hour later, there's the fluffy duck man and three or four fancily-dressed friends all enjoying a well-earned cuppa, sitting together in the window. So John and Stephanie go over to them while I attempt to organise our departure with Nora and Molly. But the trouble is Open House now seems to be full of people I happen to know, so it must be about ten minutes later when I'm finally moving towards the door with my two friends. All this time John and Stephanie have been talking to the collectors, and suddenly one of them comes up to me.

It's the pink fluffy duck man, and he asks me seriously, 'Please could I have a private word with you?' I notice he's looking rather tearful. *Oh no*, I think, *I bet he's got marriage problems and someone here has told him I might help.*

'I'm really sorry,' I say, 'but could we make an appointment, because you see I've these children and. . . .'

'Yes, I know,' he interrupts, 'that's why I'm here. One of them is mine!'

'*Wha-a-a-t!*' I gasp, stunned. But suddenly I notice his eyes. And I know he's right; they're exactly like John's uniquely hazy-blue ones.

'You see,' he explains, 'your little lad's been talking to us for the last ten minutes. Then he suddenly asked me my name, so I told him: George Carter. His little sister said, "Oh, John used to be called Wayne Stephen Carter." And immediately I knew. I haven't seen him for ten years, since around his first birthday, and then no one thought he was going to survive, his heart being so bad . . . and I just can't believe it!' he sighs, as tears begin to roll down his deliriously happy face.

And neither can I. Out of half a million people in Sheffield, John has found his long-lost dad all on his own, without even looking, at an age when many adopted children start desperately desiring to know their roots. We'd never known anything about John's parents, who split up soon after he was born. And, as George says, he lives right over the other side of the city and he's never been near Open House before this Saturday afternoon's charity collection.

It amazes me to think, too, that if we'd left one minute earlier, George would have been talking to his own son for all that time and would never have known! I feel like flinging my arms around him and inviting him back home there and then, certain that only the Lord could arrange such a surprise. But at the same time I'm half-worrying that George might want John back. And I know I can't ask him to our house, anyway, until David is in the know! Another father might just seem one too many to David. Though, in my heart, I'm sure he's going to be as thrilled as I am. So just what do I say, I wonder, lost for words? But not for long!

Ever since John came to us at nearly two, after living in the children's hospital from six weeks on, we've prayed for his natural parents (then separated) to meet the Lord. So it suddenly occurs to me to ask a strange question, as George and I look incredulously from each other to John, still chatting unawares to his fancy friends. 'You've not been born again, by any chance?' I enquire. And George's face immediately lights up.

'Oh yes! I remarried seven years ago, and my wife's friend took us to Copper Street Pentecostal, and I gave my life straight to the Lord. And you too?' he beams.

And beaming is exactly what David does back home a little while later, with a delighted John, as I tell them all about George and who he is. John's heard from us about his 'other mum and dad' ever since he was old enough to understand, and has often joined us in praying for them too. So we're soon making arrangements for George and Susan and John's new six-year-old step-sister, Gemma, to come over.

'You are lucky, Johnny, having two dads,' says Stephanie.

'No, I'm not,' replies John smiling triumphantly. 'I've not got two dads, I've got three!'

Well, the Lord has answered my early-morning prayer about no more 'neighbours' for a while with a mind-blowing 'no!'. But he's proved to us again that when he's in charge we can afford to laugh at our fears. And we can trust him to work out our relationships too, if we're willing to love with his love. So we're certainly ready for him to arrange for us to find John's mum if that's right, though at the moment she seems lost from the map.

Loving our neighbour really is the only way to live once God is running our lives. And though my feelings might sometimes be shouting out in exasperation, 'Who needs neighbours?' my heart knows we *all* do. For our sakes as well as theirs—at home, at church, on the move, and wherever we are. We all need neighbours, good and bad, to learn to love with Jesus' love. He didn't say, 'Choose your neighbour,' just, 'Love him, whoever he is.' And as Christians we're not allowed to be put off by appearance, or colour, or disability, or class. It's part of carrying our cross and dying to ourselves. But it's part of knowing the joy of the Lord, too, as we discover what he can do when we're willing to put ourselves out for anyone he sends. That's what our family and friends have found over and over again through the years. So read on if you need encouragement over what can happen for your 'neighbours', too—whoever they are.

PART ONE
Neighbours

1

Too Close for Comfort

It wasn't so much a case of strange bedfellows that Friday morning. More like strange 'step-mothers', to be literally accurate. There we were, two mothers who'd never met before and who would normally have been worlds apart. But we both sat weeping together on our front door-step in the bright summer sunshine, as my new gypsy friend shared her story with me. We were as different as chalk and cheese, her nut-brown, crinkly complexion and colourful clothes making my pale face and denims seem downright drab. But as Rosie slowly opened her heart to me that morning we couldn't have been closer. And as I listened I was ashamed to think of how much I'd resented her presence ten minutes before.

I'd been writing against the clock when she arrived. There were just two hours to go before I had to go to Radio Hallam in the centre of Sheffield and record five short 'Thoughts for the Day' on faith—and I still needed to put the last two 'thoughts' and their accompanying stories on paper. The children were safely at school, but the elderly ladies enjoying a cup of coffee with my mother in the front room, plus the phone and our ever-open door, all meant my writing was likely to be rather interrupted. And so it was.

When the door-bell rang for the third time since I'd started to pen my inspiration, I was tempted to pretend I was out. But as my mother's voice drifted from the door through to the dining room, I realised someone wanted to sell us something, and that I'd better rescue my kind-hearted mum quickly. And anyway, I'd prayed as I washed the breakfast dishes that God would only allow the interruptions he knew would fit with my finishing on time to record those radio slots. So though I couldn't help sighing at how fine he seemed to be cutting it, I knew I'd really no option but to trust him; not if I was going to hear him well enough to write what people needed to hear over the air next week.

My sigh quickly turned to one of relief, though, when I saw a slight, weather-beaten figure standing at the door with her basket over one arm. It would only take a minute to buy a bit of lace and then be back to my pen-pushing again. Or would it . . . ?

'If you don't mind, I'll just sit myself down on your doorstep, lady.' The gypsy smiled wearily at me. 'I'm just feeling a bit weak. But I've got some lovely, delicate lace here.'

'How much is the cheapest, please?' I enquired resentfully, quite ready for my roaming doorstep-saleswoman to tell me that she had a dozen dependent children half-starved at home, a husband dying in hospital, and a bag full of wonderful lacy bargains at only £5 each. But I was wrong. The gypsy's fine fingers held up hair-ribbon lengths of beautiful creamy lace at only 25p a piece. As she said it, though, I suddenly noticed pain in her eyes, and I couldn't help offering her a comforting cup of coffee—against all my inclinations.

'That would be very kind, lady,' she replied gratefully, but she refused my invitation to come in and join the front-room get-together (while I whizzed back to my writing). So as I encouraged her to help herself to sugar and biscuits a minute later, I was hoping she'd be happy instead to enjoy the warm refreshing solitude of the front steps. Then she could get her strength back for five minutes and I could catch up with the timetable. But it wasn't to be. Just as I turned away from giving our grateful guest a cushion she asked me a mind-blowing question: 'Are you a real Christian, lady?'

By now I'd discovered her name, and that she travelled the country a great deal. And I could guess why she'd asked the question—there was a little 'Jesus is the Way' sticker on our door. But the fact that Rosie knew there were real Christians as well as the pseudo-sort had me stopped in my tracks. Ignoring the beckoning back-room, I remembered hearing about how gypsies are becoming born again all over Europe, especially during the last few years. 'Was Rosie one of them?' I wondered. So I asked her.

'No, lady, I can't be,' she answered, sadly. And immediately I knew that even if the two radio 'God-spots' consisted of my saying, 'I just want you to know that Jesus loves you. And now perhaps you'd like to think about that for the next two minutes and forty-five seconds,' then so be it. Especially since Rosie's salvation had to matter more than my radio reputation. And, anyway, meeting people's needs like Rosie's was what my broadcasting was all about. So I sat down beside her on the step and heard why being a believer was beyond her.

Rosie's very first words both saddened and cheered me. 'You see, lady'—I couldn't induce her to call me Hilary—'I'm not able to be a real Christian because there's someone I can't forgive.'

If only some church people could see as clearly as Rosie, I thought, *about God's conditions for kingdom living—because now we can pray the barrier out of the way, and maybe soon be sisters!*

But then Rosie told me about her daughter-in-law's involvement in the occult, and how it had led to two of her six grandchildren being given to other gypsies. And on top of that their mother despised her husband, Rosie's son, so much that she'd caused other travellers to beat him up, and to maltreat his children too—such sadness and cruelty soon had me shedding tears with Rosie as I sat with my arm around her. If I'd not known Jesus, I don't see how I'd have been able to forgive that daughter-in-law either, so how was I to help Rosie?

A very effective prayer that I've discovered over the years is also a very short one. So I prayed it silently, but loud and clear, to my Maker. And 'Help, Father!' soon had me seeing sense for Rosie. 'You know, Rosie, until you've forgiven your daughter-in-law, your prayers for your son and grandchildren—for their protection and blessing—just won't be as effective as they could be. So though it's tremendously hard to forgive her, it's tremendously worth it. And then your prayers can change her, too!'

Fetching a Bible, and asking Mum and her friends in the front-room to pray, I showed Rosie the verse about our needing to forgive before God can forgive us (Mark 11:25). It wasn't long before Rosie was asking the Lord for power to forgive her daughter-in-law, and receiving that power too. And very soon after that I'd a new sister sitting with me on the step, as Rosie asked Jesus to take over her life. Since she couldn't read at all, I just pencilled our address and phone number on the front of a Christian magazine, for a literate gypsy friend to read to her (along with the contents), so she'd remember where we lived next time she was in the area.

Knowing how much opposition Rosie could be meeting for her new-found faith, I explained about being filled to overflowing with the Holy Spirit, too. Then Rosie asked for the fire and the peace of the Holy Spirit's filling to fall on her. Or rather, I did the asking, and she did the receiving—which led to her asking for prayer for her chronic problems of tiredness (due to an underactive thyroid); and then to thanking Jesus for the healing he'd already claimed for her at Calvary.

When we stood together on the step saying goodbye ten minutes later, it was wonderful to see Rosie beaming with joy. The last I saw of her, she was walking energetically up the road, waving her magazine at me. And that was the last I saw of anyone for nearly an hour, while my thoughts, and the ink, flowed on the subject of faith and the power of forgiveness—thanks to Rosie.

As I drove into town to the studios she was still on my mind. Especially the fact that I'd almost turned her away. 'Lord, why is it,' I asked him, 'that the close encounters you bring about with people who're becoming ready to meet you, always seem so uncomfortable and inconvenient to start with?'

And as I arrived at Radio Hallam it seemed as if he was saying to me that his love is best broadcast through us when we're not relying on our own human affection for someone—because we have very little or none of it to give, compared with him. So we have to rely on his convicting, converting, life-changing love instead. And that makes all the difference. But sometimes it's really hard to realise—especially when God's arranging for us to relate to the sort of neighbours we'd rather do without.

Like, for instance, the neighbours around me in the seedy flat I found for myself as a student, when my friends went off for their long summer vacations.

We poor dental students had to stay behind for our clinical work, so I temporarily left the student hall of residence for cheap inner-city accommodation. The bedsit below me contained a beefy young man, with a Dracula smile and bad breath, who played loud rock music all night and slept all day—except when he heard me coming downstairs, that is. However quietly I tip-toed, his ESP seemed to tell him when to leap out at me with proposals of undying love, if only I would sew on a button for him, write a letter to his mum, or show him how to boil an egg!

The nearest neighbour I've ever had, though, was when I arrived as a scared new student in Leeds, billeted to a little back-street terraced house with a landlady who was Thora Hird's double—but only in appearance. I very quickly realised that I was only there on sufferance, for the money. Mrs Platt's mother can never have taught her how to boil an egg, either. So I enjoyed a compul-sory crash diet, crash-landing from ten stone to eight-and-a-half in no time at all with the help of soggy dumplings, burned cabbage and lumpy sago. The saving grace was that we students ate on our own in the back while Mrs Platt enjoyed hers on a tray in front of the telly. I can only assume that her long practice in downing that impossible diet left her enjoyment unimpaired by any memory of a real meal. Mrs P never seemed to notice the contents of the paper bags secreted in her dustbin. Perhaps that was why her cats were so fat.

Anyway, soon after arriving in her polished palace that first night—she was very good at polishing—I discovered I wasn't alone. 'The other young lady arrived very punctually,' said Mrs P, with a pursed smile, hinting at my besetting sin. 'She's upstairs, and it's nearly bedtime so you might as well go up—and take Rosemary's cocoa too. It's a very nice bed you've got. I've not had it long.'

I was more interested in meeting Rosemary than in meeting the bed. 'Hope we're going to get on, Lord,' I breathed as I climbed the steep, narrow staircase to Rosemary's room. Mrs P suddenly came up behind me, and as Rosemary opened the door to us my heart sank to hear Mrs P say, 'It always helps, that's what I say, sharing a room, for getting on together.' Rosemary winked across at me reassuringly as Mrs P rambled on about 'no men allowed on the premises', and I tried to reciprocate, except that I've never quite mastered the art of winking! But there was rapport between us right from the start. 'Oh well, getting on with Rosemary should be no trouble, even if we do have to share a room,' I realised. But I wasn't prepared for Mrs P's next remark as I stood halfway behind the door.

'I know it's only a three-quarter bed, but then neither of you are too big, and it's the very best quality spring-interior.' Aghast, I peered round the door to see what she was talking about. Surely she didn't mean it? But she did. And I was horrified. My previously over-protected rather private self was going to be sharing an inadequate bed with a perfect stranger. Rosemary looked much too tall for it and I was certainly too plump. But worst of all, the sight of the bed suddenly made me remember that I had to kneel down and pray—as I'd promised the Lord I would do before I left home—in front of someone who'd probably laugh her head off.

Anyone would have thought—from my state of nerves at the fast-approaching prayer time—that I was in a packed barracks instead of just sharing a bed with a demure student of French! I slowed down my preparations for bed so much, in the hope that Rosemary would be fast asleep before I was ready to pray, that she must have wondered whether dental students were obliged to clean their teeth for ten minutes every night! But she wasn't a fast mover either, and I was dismayed to see her still up when I crept back into the room. But not for long, because suddenly Rosemary wasn't up any more—but down on her knees praying to the Lord whom she knew better than I did. She must have had a shock to find I was suddenly kneeling down beside her too.

After that I guess we were talking until two in the morning, and as time went on we found we had almost no trouble at all obeying those basic instructions to 'love your neighbour as yourself'.

It seems to me that the only possible reason Jesus used the standard 'as much as you love yourself' in giving us our instructions is that it applies equally to us all. If he'd said, 'as much as you love your best friend,' then the variations would be vast. But the Lord knows that we all have the same basic drive to put ourselves first, and that however unselfish we become, we still naturally notice ourselves and our needs all the time, whether we're confident and self-possessed, or depressed and sorry for ourselves. Looking after our own interests first comes equally naturally to us all.

So neighbourliness basically boils down to, 'Do as you would be done by.' And we won't manage it unless we enrol in God's 'doing-each-other-good' school, because in his school we each have an absolutely brilliant and understanding personal tutor—the Holy Spirit. The Holy Spirit's direction as to whose needs are meant to be coming first at any given moment is totally essential, or else we'll soon run ourselves into the ground with all the needs around us. But as he shows us over and over, through circumstances, and through inner witness, whether our needs or our neighbours' (and which neighbours') are meant to be uppermost, we'll find ourselves being used for the maximum good with a minimum of fuss.

As we obey his instructions for blessing each other— which often involve denying ourselves, as Jesus made clear—we discover more and more of his supernatural power to love our neighbours the way he says. And love can keep on winning, even when our feelings are horribly negative. It's taken me a long time to realise that the Lord doesn't need us to feel good about loving our neighbours. He just needs us to get on with doing it—in prayer and in action. And whether we're the helper or the helped, the despised or the respected, love means being available for anyone at all, as God works out his divine assignments for each relationship given to him.

It doesn't matter whether our 'neighbour' is our

husband or wife, parent or child, workmate or fellow student, well-heeled neighbour or neighbourhood down-and-out. He can pour ample supplies of his love into our emptiness, as long as we're willing to get on with simply obeying him in our relationships.

This usually involves five basic ground rules if we are to discover the freedom of loving our neighbours more and more as ourselves—whoever they are. And whether they like us or not!

1. Accept people just as they are—just as Jesus does (especially powerful therapy for failing husbands or wives).

2. Put yourself in the other person's place, imagining how you might be if life, genetics and upbringing had dealt with you as they have with them.

3. Ask Jesus to show you more of your faults (maybe adding to the relationship difficulties), as you compare yourself with him instead of with the other person.

4. Forgive them any hurt they might ever have caused. And ask their forgiveness, if necessary, too.

5. Make a list of every good thing about your neighbour, down to the very last detail, even like 'being fond of animals'. Go through that list morning and night, thanking God, and praying for the person to be blessed body, soul and spirit.

Very soon you could be adding to the list and seeing a whole new neighbour emerge. And even if your neighbour still somehow manages to stay exactly the same, you'll change so much that the situation will, too. And you'll be able to be totally clear-sighted as you apply these well-known words to your relationship situations: 'Lord, give me the courage to change what can be changed, the serenity to accept what can't, and the wisdom to know the difference.' It's a good thing I've learned those words by heart, because I know that I'm going to have many more opportunities to put them into practice. That's if my past is anything to go by!

2

Who Knows? Heaven Knows!

There are some neighbours we're able to help practically in all sorts of ways. We keep finding ourselves in the right place at the right time to aid them in their troubles, and to pass on plenty of blessings. But sharing with them the greatest gift there is—the present that lasts for ever—somehow seems impossible. And though we know we're talking with them about a matter of life and death, when the opportunity arises to share our faith (if we actually dare to take it), they never seem quite able to grasp the lifeline we're throwing out. I can't express too much surprise over that fact, though, as I was so slow to do the very same thing!

My inability to grasp God's good news really began when I was a pre-teen in the Girls' Brigade. The GB motto always used to puzzle me, and because I was an extra-conscientious sort of child, I used to worry each week as we recited together our motto 'to save life'. I could cope with the law and the promise which came first, but wondered anxiously how I was ever actually going to manage to save a life. When was I going to find someone about to drown, near enough to the bank for me to pull him out? I wasn't a very good swimmer. Or when might I be fortunate enough to find an old lady whose house was only slightly ablaze, and whom I could rescue without getting singed myself? I'd managed to keep up with all the other ever-increasing challenges in gaining the GB badges, but I didn't see how I was possibly going to fulfil that motto without pushing someone in, or lighting the match myself!

It wasn't until shortly before I became a very young GB captain as a new student in Leeds, on a run-down housing estate, that I realised 'to save life' was alluding to the eternal sort! All through my childhood I'd presumed that everyone must be going to heaven (except, of course, Hitler and his henchmen) because God is bound to be kind to everyone in the end—isn't he? Then at a schoolgirls' camp during my teens I suddenly understood how he was so very kind to me that he'd allowed his perfect and beloved Son to take the punishment that was coming to me. Jesus wasn't only cruelly tortured and killed, but at the same time he experienced all the greed, evil and perversion of God's fallen, 'me first' creation.

Now that we have sons of our own, I don't know how God did it, except that he's given me a clue in allowing me to taste a little of that amazing love that kept Jesus in untold agony on the cross for every person on this planet. And so have all who have ever been willing to hand over their lives to this astonishing elder Brother. He's the Brother who defeated sin, death and Satan at Calvary, so we can go free—free from the everlasting home in hell that the devil hopes will begin for us here and now—the moment that we hand our lives over to Jesus who sets us 'free indeed' (John 8:36, AV).

It was such a relief to know he was running my life, as I ran that GB Company. Half the girls there had relations in trouble with the police, or were halfway there themselves. But I was able to shift the responsibility of it all into the safe hands of my heavenly Father, who could miraculously change their lives where I hadn't a hope; and every now and again, since that glorious discovery, I've found new neighbours of every age, ready and waiting to be introduced to the Father they've not yet met themselves.

But plenty of people are in need of practical or emotional support, without feeling any spiritual need at all. In John 3:3, Jesus says that unless we are born again we can't even see God's kingdom. And maybe the most important 'seeing' begins when we realise what we're missing. But for those neighbours who don't even begin to see, we just need to keep being available until maybe they do. There's no way we can help everyone in our neighbourhood in practical need, but as we ask the Lord to lead us to those we can help the most, it will sometimes happen that 'new lives for old' will be part of the result. But even when it isn't, we can keep on going the second mile with the same person over and over, with God's love fuelling our response even to 3 am 'emergency' phone calls! And we can stay that way, speaking the truth in love for as long as he needs—even when the truth becomes, 'I'm sorry, I can't help you any more.' But there will always be more neighbours in need on God's agenda, waiting to be found.

Finding them was something I just couldn't do when we first came to live here. However hard I looked, there just didn't seem to *be* any needy neighbours! The population around us has aged considerably since, but at that time everyone seemed young, fit and independent. So I asked the health visitor who followed-up new little Elinor whether she knew any lonely old people. 'Oh yes, plenty,' she smiled, and immediately found me four to be going on with.

The first one decided she wasn't lonely after all if I was bringing children with me (even though they were brought up, happily but strictly, by James Dobson's methods, a decade before this brilliant Christian child psychologist's books hit Britain). The second one, Stan, was almost bedridden and riddled with excruciating arthritis. He swore like a trooper, but taught me plenty about ignoring adversity and letting mind rule over matter. 'No matter,' he'd mutter, every time anything defeated him, turning to the next task in hand. It often was 'in hand' too, because he was always writing poetry. He'd painfully clutch his pen and scrawl a line or two more of the ode he was currently working on, often dedicated to his long-suffering home-help! He wrote for her a lot because his language, his temper, and his ability to pinch bottoms, when he was in the mood, meant she was often on the point of resigning. To make it worse, his budgie had learned to swear quite fluently, which meant that Stan's house was always a favourite port of call for Matt, Ellie and then, later, little Lucy.

The children were all celebrated in verse too, each birthday. I never quite understood why I wasn't, except that religious verse wasn't his scene, and he quickly realised I was 'worse than the vicar'! I never discovered whether Stan saw the light before he left this earth, from his hospital bed. It's a light that he partly mirrored in the way he never ever complained, although in constant pain. But I learned to leave Stan and his after-life with the Lord who loved him far more than I ever could.

And I had to do likewise with Mrs 'Oggy-Goggy' (Elinor's rendering of Mrs Rogers). She was a gruff Yorkshire great-grandma with a very soft-centred heart where children were concerned. It was a relief that the children's teeth were well-fluoridated, in view of the vast number of jelly babies and chocolate buttons they consumed at her house. But though she was so sweet to the children she felt very bitter towards certain neighbours and relations from her past. And I was never sure she understood the Lord's words about needing to forgive before we could be forgiven ourselves.

The last of the four to be visited came first in the amount of fun and faith-stretching she initiated. Miss Polly Swinden was the youngest of twelve Victorian children born to the family of a master craftsman in one of Sheffield's numerous cutlery firms. The children all made their own way in the world, except for Polly who stayed at home, like so many youngest daughters, to care for her parents in their declining years. She had the intellect to have risen as far as some of her relatives who escaped the steel works to win university and research posts, through 'new-fangled' evening classes. But Polly confined her ingenuity to inventing—in a way that would have impressed Heath Robinson the crazily inventive cartoonist—particularly the pulley system she'd improvised for transporting her hot-water bottle upstairs to the back bedroom of her little terraced house, when old age left her creaking joints struggling to carry it up. So I was delighted to visit Polly, except for one thing—her inventive ingenuity with food I could definitely have done without!

Once a week I called after school with the children to fetch her shopping, and we could never escape without a dainty afternoon tea, served in a polite Victorian manner. The children soon learned to cope with their unaccustomed cups and saucers, but they had awful trouble swallowing the accompanying delicacies. The problem was that Polly always concocted a special spread from a base of semi-solid soured milk and whatever other little additions she'd saved from her left-overs, like shredded spinach, or macerated mince, as she gloried in never throwing away a single grain of 'good' food. So each week she surprised us with a new delicacy on her homemade rusks. Each week, too, I made excuses for our offspring while I smilingly forced down more than my share, knowing that feeding us was the highlight of Polly's week.

There was one special 'Aunty Polly afternoon' though that is for ever the highlight of our children's otherwise rather unwilling visits. It all began a few weeks before, really, when Polly fell awkwardly in her higgledy-piggledy house and hurt one of her eyes so badly that she was in hospital for a few days. Sadly she had to lose the eye and was fitted with an artificial one. When she came home she was very eager to see me because she had an unusual request.

'Hilary, I wish you'd have a look at my eye. Could you just take it out and check with the instructions that it's in right, because it does feel funny. Look, here's its little box with the leaflet about how to put it in.' I swallowed hard and stalled for time, but changing the conversation did no good at all; even asking about the latest soured-milk surprise had no useful effect. It was a case of 'love your neighbour' or nothing! So five minutes later I

steeled myself, took a deep breath, perused the instructions and, as so often happens with fears and phobias,
found there was nothing to it when once I'd made up
my mind. Extracting the eye was no trouble compared
to extracting teeth! And I knew exactly the same relief
as some of my patients who've been petrified to present
themselves for treatment, but who've gone ahead and
found the worry beforehand is a billion times worse
than ever the actuality could be.

So removing that glass eye proved to be as easy as
winking, and really eye-opening too! Because until then
I'd always thought glass eyes were like marbles, but I
discovered they're actually pear-shaped with the
pointed end fitting into the loose tissue by the bridge of
the nose; and amazingly I found the cause of her
discomfort was that she'd had a left-sided eye fitted into
her right-sided socket, the wrong way up so that it
looked normal. No wonder it felt uncomfortable.

'That's fine,' she pronounced dismissively as I finished
replacing it properly. When I showed her in the mirror
that it might feel fine, but it made her look totally tipsy,
with a vast expanse of mal-positioned white above the
tiny two millimetres of visible blue pupil, she hardly
bothered to look. 'I don't go out at all,' she reminded
me, 'so why should I care what I look like, as long as I'm
comfy? And I am now, thank you very much. So that's
the end of that.' And although I tried my hardest to take
Polly on a return visit to the hospital for a replacement,
she was adamant that her embarrassing glass eye was
there to stay.

And so it was, except for one memorable afternoon
which the children will never forget. We were all sitting
around Aunty Polly's Victorian table, complete with

antique lace cloth, and delicacies to match. I silently thanked the Lord for my cast-iron digestion, and for Polly's one concession to modernity—the television set, which she kept on from dawn to dusk. I always timed our visits after school to coincide with *Play School* to keep the offspring relatively 'seen and not heard' in a proper Victorian manner. Polly had taken the kettle off the hob and was decorously pouring out the tea when suddenly we all jumped with surprise. She had emitted the most enormous sneeze, and we looked up just in time to see that glass eye fly through the air and land neatly and tidily right in her own well-filled cup! It was a wonder the children's eyes didn't pop out of their heads too. Being a woman of great poise and resource, Polly picked up her teaspoon, fished out her eye, polished it on her apron, and popped it back in place without a word! All done in the twinkling of an eye, and with total disregard for any vulgarly giggling infants.

Despite Polly's 'properness' she could also let her hair down (both literally and metaphorically) when she was in the mood, and possessed a fund of old family jokes to entertain us with. A favourite—maybe because she never quite got on with the church—was about a bishop. It went like this:

Little boy: 'I'm glad the bishop came to our church today.'

Mother (having explained beforehand about the bishop's crook and his being a shepherd of the flock): 'Why's that, dear?'

Little boy: 'Well, I'm glad the bishop came because now I know what a real crook looks like.'

I never did manage to entice Polly to church, and I never seemed able to share my faith in a way that made sense to her either. But I enjoyed her friendship for eight years, before she suffered yet another fall and developed pneumonia in hospital. She might still have pulled through except for one snag—the staff always called her Polly instead of Miss Swinden. Being on first-name terms was seen as a reassuring comfort for disorientated old people. But it didn't seem at all like that to politely Victorian Polly. Even I never became more familiar than writing 'Miss S' on the scribbled notes I sometimes left her in passing. The children were allowed to call her Aunty Polly, but that's as far as it went. The nurses just didn't seem able to see Polly's point of view when I tried to explain. So Polly thought they were making fun of her, turned her face to the wall, and never recovered.

God was very kind to me and allowed me to arrive at her hospital bed just before she passed on. She seemed unconscious, but I arrived unknowingly at just the right moment to be with her and to pray in the heavenly language the Lord had recently supplied me with, not knowing how else to pray for Polly as she prepared to depart this life. And I won't know till I do likewise whether she did surrender her life to the Lord whom I'd tried to share with her all those years. But I thank God anyway for the privilege of knowing Polly and learning so much from her grit, ingenuity and great love of life. I'll just have to leave her, with so many others I've known, to the Father who always knows best.

He knows best too about just how to win people from darkness and despair into the light and love of becoming a new creation. Whenever I try to do it myself it always shows—by the mess I leave behind! The mess of embarrassed friends, fleeing acquaintances, and even

WHO KNOWS? HEAVEN KNOWS!

sometimes scoffing foes. But when I let God guide me as to the right time to introduce someone to Jesus, the opportunity can take a lot longer to arrive than I expect, but I discover it's *just* the right time for that particular person. Only God can see into a human heart and know exactly when that heart is ready to surrender to him, despite what outward appearances might be saying to us. And often he doesn't need to use any particular person at all to win a neighbour to himself—just a lot of links in a chain, who are often oblivious to what is happening.

Margaret Cundiff—the well-known broadcaster and author—tells how someone heard her speak about faith on the radio and felt led to write and share how she acquired hers. The listener had become so depressed after her husband died that she ceased all contact with friends and neighbours and just lay in bed for much of the day feeling suicidally sorry for herself. One day, dragging herself to the kitchen for a cup of tea, she noticed a painter working on her neighbour's garage doors and realised what a sadly peeling state hers were in. Somehow she felt motivated enough, knowing winter was coming on, to tap on the window and beckon the painter over to see if he could cope with her garage doors too.

A month or so later, when he was able to fit them in, the before-and-after contrast made her feel she must have the whole house painted. Contact with the painter as he decorated the inside of her house, gave her confidence to go to a church coffee morning she'd been given a leaflet about recently. And that visit led gradually to church attendance, then to arranging the altar flowers, and to visiting lonely, housebound people. All that activity accompanied a gradual surrender to God and a realisation that she had even more to give now a living Lord Jesus was running her life—her money! She had £100 she could spare and was wondering about dividing it between the church and the RSPCA when her vicar preached about abandoned children in Korea and how donations could be the means of 'adopting' a child in need over there for care, food and schooling to be supplied, through sending £8 a month. So that's just what she did, and now no one can recognise her as the depressed lady of the year before at all, as she and her 'new child' write to each other and she prays for him, and for many other people too.

It's so often insignificant seeming links in a chain that help neighbours to meet the Person who gives real meaning to life, and the joy that goes with him, even though we often have no idea for a long time, if at all, that anything is happening. So let's make sure we're the right link, in the right place, at the right time. That's something only our Managing Director can arrange. As we keep putting him first, he manages our lives in the most incredible way, directing us to exactly the right people at just those right times when we're able to supply their needs. And to direct them straight to him too. It all depends on our obedience. But when obeying him becomes the most exciting thing we ever do, over and over, all day long, the results of that obedience become unforgettable. So unforgettable that sometimes neither we, nor our neighbours, can quite believe our eyes.

3

Fast Forward

It's a continual surprise to me that all sorts of people at work, on the bus, or even at church, talk about characters in the BBC's *Neighbours* as though they're intimate friends. But from long experience I've found that people who know almost everything about the casts of the television soaps often have no interest at all in their own neighbours. In fact they might not even know their names.

That's exactly how it is with one elderly neighbour who spends a lot of time at our home. She has a great relationship with the television, but there's no way we can induce her to visit any of the other lonely old ladies around the neighbourhood. So it was a lovely surprise to hear Mabel say the other day, 'Well, I'll just go and see Mrs Jones.' Our joy was short-lived, though, as Mabel went upstairs instead of outside, and we realised 'Mrs Jones' was an old family euphemism for the toilet.

I suppose it isn't surprising, whatever our age, that fictional neighbours are so much safer and more interesting than the real sort (unless there is scandal involved). The latter can often cause us inconvenience, and even trouble, especially if they are housebound and needing help, or noisy and preventing our sleep. But stumbling-blocks can soon turn into stepping-stones towards even more satisfying relationships when we're willing to love whomever God sends with the love only he can supply. That love means we have to be willing to keep on bearing each other's burdens and to speak the truth in love as well—especially to those noisy neighbours. Soon we'll be discovering good points we never knew they had.

But sometimes God doesn't want us to do any speaking at all if our trouble is a neighbour who ignores us. Maybe the reason is great shyness, or grief over some matter. Maybe differences in the past have caused the neighbour to give up on relationships altogether. Or maybe they just think they're too good for us, or that we're too good for them! But whichever way it is, God needs us to keep on loving those people, praying for them, and noticing any opportunity God gives us to offer love unobtrusively—from a smile to maybe being in the right place at the right time to open their gate when they're returning home laden with shopping. But we do have to respect their privacy, and if they want to keep ignoring us, we have no right to force ourselves on them in any way that needs a response. Our continuing, caring prayer, in any case, will accomplish far more than words where they're not wanted. And the social and spiritual rape of forcing ourselves on people who are not wanting to relate to us—or to God either—will do far more harm than good.

If our lives revolve around ourselves we won't be able to accept people who reject us. But if our lives revolve around Jesus we'll increasingly find their rejection will keep on fuelling our commitment to secret prayer each time we see them—and at other times too, if the Lord encourages us that way. And if we're feeling sure there must be another way we could help, we only need to ask God to show us how. If he doesn't show us anything new, we can be content that our prayer is all he needs. But whatever sort of neighbours we have there's no joy like seeing them meet the Person who can sort everything out perfectly, as my friend Kath found out.

'Since I've lived here,' she told me, 'I've had some lovely opportunities to pray with people.' Kath is a retired minister's wife who lives a few hundred yards further up our very long road. She's a person whose beautiful smile must be as powerful a Christian witness to her neighbours as all the expertise she has gained in ministry over the years. 'The prayers just happened naturally,' Kath continued, 'as I've grown to know people and needs have arisen. Sometimes it's a family crisis that is the cause, or sometimes a need for inner healing—and praying with people is a wonderful way to introduce them to Jesus. It's like prayer-evangelism. People could be put off by a direct appeal to turn to Jesus, but a need which has us pray together can soon bring us both face-to-face with the living Lord who loves us.'

Kath's experience certainly tallies with mine. Caring prayer, two to One, can communicate the love of Jesus faster than anything else. For instance, it's a bit difficult to introduce the fact of Jesus' love into a conversation about cooking, or clothes, or the weather. And becoming adept at bringing Jesus into every conversation can be a great turn-off when God isn't giving the green light. For most people, there's no interest in Christian things

anyway until there is a need that is too big for anyone
but God. But then it's amazing how powerfully God
often seems to respond to the tiniest request from a
person who's not yet met him personally, as he begins to
point them in his direction. Those of us who've known
him for years, though, can often find his answers
materialising much more slowly as he teaches us to trust
him, whatever happens, and as he feeds us meat instead
of milk. But we can still be thrilled by the speed of his
answers for others!

One such person was Pauline, from the next road,
who asked me to have the fellowship meeting pray for
her when she went into hospital for a hysterectomy. We
only prayed a simple little prayer against the pain and
for Pauline's recovery and signed a get well card for her
at the beginning of the meeting, while the request was
still fresh in people's minds. Then I didn't meet Pauline
again for a month. And when I did she took my breath
away by saying, 'I never felt one moment's pain during
all my hospitalisation!' I don't know who was more
surprised—Pauline, the hospital staff, or I—but Pauline,
with the rest of us, knew exactly whom to thank.

And then there was the neighbour's dog from the
bottom of the garden. We're blessed with lots of extra
neighbours, as our long garden stretches from the main
road to a side street, providing a useful short cut for
people in a hurry to reach the bus-stop near our front
gate. The garden also provides plenty of extra territory
for all the nomadic cats and dogs of the district. But the
particular dog in my story, a friendly black doormat, was
safely on his lead that sunny day, taking his owner for
their daily constitutional! The lady was looking so
unhappy as we approached each other that I asked after

her health. 'It's not me; it's Scamp,' she replied, wiping away a tear. 'The vet's just told me that he's only three months to live. It's a growth, you see.'

Instantly my mind flashed back to the book I'd just finished reading. It was the story of an American dairy farmer's discovery of Life with a capital J, and the enormous international organisation he founded when Jesus entered his life bringing countless businessmen, worldwide, to know Jesus too. In the middle of his book, *The Happiest People on Earth*, Demos Shakarian recounts how thousands of his dairy cattle were about to be slaughtered because of a deadly virus when the simple but powerful prayer of a visiting evangelist saw them all healed at once!

If God can heal a whole herd of desperately ill cows simultaneously, I thought to myself, *then one little dog won't be any trouble to him at all.* I knew I'd sound very simplistic to Scamp's owner, but the Bible tells us to be like little children in our faith, so I accepted the challenge and told her.

'God can heal animals as well as people, you know, because of Jesus. So I'm going to pray for Scamp to get better, and perhaps you could do the same. Because if you've just enough faith to pray, then that's more than enough faith to see a miracle happen!' And maybe she did have. And maybe she learned a whole lot more about the Lord's love through Scamp because every time we met after that Scamp looked more and more healthy. Three years later he was still taking his mistress for a walk, full of that dogged determination to enjoy life— and fit as a fiddle! It must be sweet music in God's ears when any part of his creation, human or not, is contributing to that symphony of wholeness he's designed us all to play in. Especially when the harmony between neighbours produces chords of love that can reverberate far and near.

But of course, the basic beat is the most important part of the symphony. And if such a symphony is to catch our imagination—and continue—that beat has to be the heartbeat of real love, self-denying love, love that not only prays but has us put ourselves out for people too. Being a good neighbour means being ready over and over to go the second mile, even when people don't deserve it. Along with that necessary grace, we also need wisdom to know when 'no' is the right response—for the other person's sake as well as ours. Especially if selfish over-indulgence is crippling their existence.

Often, though, we *do* need to give away our time, lend a listening ear, share our shopping, or part with our possessions for neighbours in need. Or maybe an under-the-weather mum needs us to look after her children. And sometimes we even need to 'turn the other cheek' if, for instance, we're overhearing gossip about us being do-gooders who are neglecting our own families—as long as it's not true, of course! Or maybe loving our neighbours means apologising for our cat digging up their garden, even if their children do run riot all over ours sometimes. Because when we have given our life away to our incredibly loving Lord, forgetting ourselves can just come naturally—or supernaturally—so that we're available to him anytime, for anyone needing our help.

But relationships are always two-way, and sometimes we can find ourselves receiving more than we are giving where neighbours are concerned. It didn't look that way at first with Steve from next door, though, when he

called round on one of our more complicated
Sundays. . . .

It was a day when I hardly seemed to have a second to
spare. The phone rang so many times before church
that I only just had time for a flying visit to check on the
elderly neighbour who was ill down the road, in between
organising the children to wash up and tidy up after
breakfast, and hurrying back to find the visual aids I still
needed for Sunday School that afternoon. My class was
due to be learning about God's judgement as well as his
love, and I still needed to find half-a-dozen pictures of
cats or dogs from old magazines so they could start the
lesson by pretending to be judges at a show. But all I
could see in my old magazines were one or two rather
nondescript pet pictures, in the five minutes left to me
before switching the oven on 'low' and hurrying
everyone to the car where David was already waiting,
only slightly behind schedule for church.

Back home again an hour-and-a-half later the glow of
praising the Lord together was still doing me good (in
spite of young John and Stephanie indulging in surrep-
titious unspiritual warfare on either side of me
throughout the worship). So it occurred to me to praise
the Lord that he knew how to guide me to any concealed
dog or cat pictures. Then I searched through the
dwindling pile of magazines, ably assisted by the two
youngest, while stirring the soup with my other hand.
'Please, Lord, synchronise my tasks, and lighten my
load, too,' I prayed. David and the three eldest wouldn't
be home till just before we ate, and the phone kept on
ringing all the time, usually for them.

But two minutes later I saw my prayers answered by
my load seeming to become heavier still! 'Oh Lord, how

could you?' my spirit groaned as I turned to see Steve, our new teenage neighbour from one of next door's bedsits standing on our kitchen step. He looked as though he had a problem too. 'I asked you to *lighten* my load,' my silent conversation continued as I somehow managed to smile a welcome at Steve. 'Didn't you hear me properly? You know the dinner's already stretched to the limit, and with grandpa and great-aunty Edna, and Lucy's friend here too, there's no spare room round the table either.'

'Hilary,' began Steve, 'I'm just needing you to pray with me, urgently. Since I've really surrendered to Jesus I've realised how much my family needs setting free from spiritualism. They're in a crisis right at this moment, actually. And I'm sure you'll know how to pray.'

I realised, miserably, that I couldn't get by with the 'eyes open, cooking the dinner' prayer I was hoping would do for Steve—not if we were going to be hearing God enough to come against this stronghold of spiritualism. And hearing God was still foremost in my mind as we pulled up the kitchen stools, with the dinner on simmer, and began to pray briefly for the family Steve loves so much. As he prayed in tongues (the heavenly language God had recently released in him) I suddenly knew why hearing God was so much on my mind.

One of the most effective aids to hearing God's voice in my life has been through missing a meal, or a number of meals, to pray and praise instead. And all of a sudden I could see just how God had indeed answered my load-lightening prayers a few minutes before when Steve came in. He was even going to fit in one more item on the agenda, too, that until then had looked hopeless.

Not to mention rescuing Steve from the possible rejection of not being invited to share our usually stretchable Sunday meal!

'Steve,' I interrupted at the end of his prayer. 'I've just had a thought. You know that when we fast we can hear the Lord's voice even more clearly? Well, I'll just check whether David's happy for me to serve the dinner, but then for me to miss it. . . because if you're willing for us to fast together we could pray much more powerfully. And at the same time we could go and visit a lady in hospital whom I'd promised to see today if I could, praying in the car on the way. And with both of us praying together, when we reach Nora at the hospital then she'll be doubly blessed as well!'

I knew that Nora was in a great deal of pain, and was due to be operated on for gall bladder trouble the next day. She was a Methodist local preacher, and would be hoping I'd arrive to pray with her before the operation. Up until then, with people coming for tea straight after Sunday School, I'd been trusting God to send someone else for Nora. But after checking with David, I found he was sending me. So now all I had left to trust him for were those feline and canine photographs! The trip to the hospital gave us the right amount of time in the car to finish praying comprehensively for Steve's family, and we arrived at Nora's ward just as visiting time began.

Not knowing Nora's whereabouts on the seventh-floor ward of multi-cubicles, we were walking over to the sister's desk when an operating trolley with a patient on her way to theatre paused there. So I looked instead at the ward-list notice on the wall and pointed out the right cubicle to Steve, just beyond the trolley. As I did, though, I suddenly realised that the patient on the trolley looked strangely familiar.

'Nora!' I breathed, astonished, hurrying across with Steve close behind. She looked absolutely astounded (as well she might) and tried to sit up—a rather difficult feat on an operating trolley. 'How wonderful!' she exclaimed. 'However did you know? They've only just decided to operate today instead of tomorrow. The Lord must have sent you!' And as the porter and nurse looked on bemused we enjoyed a brief moment of prayer together for Nora's perfect safety, with praise for her renewed health through the emergency operation due to start at any minute. Then, as Nora was wheeled down to the theatre, trailing clouds of glory, we went off to the hospital lift, thrilled to bits with the Lord's brilliant timing. It became even better though as we began the descent.

We were praying out loud a PS prayer that the Lord might accomplish, even then, any healing for Nora that might help the surgeon in his work. Suddenly the lift stopped at the sixth floor and in walked a staff nurse. Being halfway through a prayer I said, 'I hope you won't mind us just finishing off praying for a friend going into theatre at this moment.' And, amazingly, the nurse answered us, with a beaming smile, 'That's great, because I'm a born-again Christian too, so I'll join in.' It certainly was the biblical two or three gathered together in his name, in a mobile prayer meeting that only he could have arranged! So we expected a wonderful recovery for Nora—which is just what she received. But the Lord had even more to teach me about neighbours helping my day to go his way. . . .

As I dropped Steve at the nearby bus-stop a few

minutes later (he'd decided to visit a friend in town), I
noticed how foggy it had become. And there was a lady
standing by the bus-stop looking very weary. 'They told
me to come to the Hallamshire Hospital,' she said, 'but
now I've found out my sister's in the Claremont Nursing
Home. Do you know if it's difficult to get to?' Well, it
was, and the fog was so bad I knew she'd never find her
way unless I took her. So I did. And on the way I found
that Mary was a traditional Catholic lady with just
enough faith to pray with me for her sister. And then, as
the Holy Spirit took over, for a whole lot more besides.
So it was a very useful but a very slow journey in the
increasingly thick fog. And when I finally arrived back
home I'd one minute left before rushing off with the
children to teach Sunday School. I'd obviously have to
forget the pet show visual aid, and just *talk* about
judging instead.

Flying in, I found David kindly finishing off the pots
in the kitchen. 'Sorry to be so late, love,' I smiled across
at him as I picked up my Sunday School bag and
checked the younger children's faces were free of
dinner. 'I'm collecting the new family from church on
my way back from Sunday School and I'll have the tea
ready for half-past five, if that suits you.' The children
were putting on their coats and I was picking up the pile
of magazines to put away as David told me his plans for
after tea. All at once I made everyone jump. 'I don't
believe it!' I cried, amazed, staring at the picture before
me. One of the magazines had suddenly fallen open at a
'Bonny Baby competition' page. There, spread out
before me, were even more engrossing subjects than
dogs or cats for our junior judges. And with three dozen
assorted infants I had all the competition pictures I

could possibly want, on just one page, all ready to tear out! I'd given up on that Sunday School visual aid, but God hadn't. And he knew just how to show me what I was missing. So thirty seconds later we were flying through the door, on our way to Sunday School at last, with me feeling as though I was floating on air all the way. And I'll never forget that heavenly lesson on how much we need God to send us neighbours in need—often just when we think we need them the least!

WORK-OUT 1
Neighbours

In love and charity with your neighbour . . .
(Book of Common Prayer)

Cross patch, draw the latch
Sit by the fire and spin.
Take a cup and drink it up
Then call your neighbours in.
(Mother Goose's Melody—1760)

1. TOO CLOSE FOR COMFORT
All about blessing your neighbour, even if:

(a) you don't seem to have time
(b) they're the last neighbour you'd choose
(c) they don't deserve to be blessed
(d) you're feeling terrible.

Read Luke 8:40–56.

(a) Which barrier seems the hardest for you personally to surmount?
(b) To what degree does their gratitude or otherwise determine our willingness to help?
(c) Should Christians ever be in à hurry? Is hurrying a sin?
(d) How much does punctuality matter?

2. WHO KNOWS? HEAVEN KNOWS!

An increasing number of our neighbours are becoming pensioners—currently 18% of the population.

Read Philippians 2:1–11.

(a) What are the special qualities we need for doing old people good?

(b) We should befriend the elderly for their own sake, not for the sake of evangelism; but with time running out for agnostic or atheist elderly friends, should we be willing to share the bad news of hell in order for the good news to be relevant?

(c) Have you any lonely housebound people living near you who are needing a visit?

(d) Are there any categories of people you find it difficult to relate to—eg, the elderly, punk-rockers, schoolteachers on open nights, people in wheelchairs? Why is this?

3. FAST FORWARD

Being frenetically busy often seems a mark of twentieth-century western civilisation, especially for working mothers.

Read Romans 12:1–2.

(a) Should Christian mothers of school-age children, and under, go out to work?

(b) How can God use and solve our having more to do than we can manage, particularly when caring about neighbours is involved?

(c) Are there 'cups' that we 'drink up'—see rhyme above—to help us cope when fast-forward life gets too stressful (or when our lives become too empty and unfulfilled) that cause us to depend on material comforts instead of Christ? How can we eliminate them?

(d) Does God being in charge of every minute of our day generally lead to miracles? Have any happened to you, or through you?

Praise Point: 'Better is a neighbour that is near than a brother far off' (Proverbs 27:10, AV).

PART TWO
Neighbours in the Family

4

Home Is Where the Heart Is

'Right, all you lazy lot,' I reminded our procrastinating offspring, 'it's nearly homework time.' The table was finally cleared after our evening meal—and almost wiped clean too, except that eight-year-old John, whose turn it was, insisted on carefully feeding the dog with every crumb he could find. He was going through a 'be kind to dumb animals' phase. And Christy (named as a new Christmas present pet) certainly isn't the type to turn up her nose at any crumb of comfort coming her way!

Through the hatch I could hear John's elder brother and sisters clanking the crockery and cutlery around as they washed the pots. Elinor and Lucy were arguing about whose turn it should really be for the washing-up, drying-up and putting-away, if only Mum's memory weren't so faulty. And Matthew was drowning them out at the sink with an interesting dirge that must have been his original rendering of the current 'top of the pops'.

The only child at all ready to apply herself intellec-tually was three-year-old Stephanie. She'd discovered an un-crumby table area and was writing gobbledegook

under a picture of a lady with purple hair. 'Shall I read it
to you?' she said. 'It says, "The bestest lady in the
world—my nursery teacher."' 'What's Miss Adams got
that I've not?' I asked her, pretending to cry. But I
didn't wait for an answer, because I suddenly noticed
John and Christy playing tug-of-war under the table
with a crumby cloth. And an ominously pot-breaking
sound was reaching my ears from the contentious
kitchen area too. As I sorted everyone out I was tempted
to revise my contribution to our 'best-about-today' spot
held half-an-hour earlier in the middle of our meal. I'll
explain what I mean.

If anyone is looking particularly glum during our
meal-times we often announce a compulsory 'b.a.t.' spot,
with an innings for everyone, whether they feel like it or
not. By the end of the batting order the 'count your
blessings' principle has usually worked—even if the best
happening was: 'That boy who smells so disgusting
being moved to another desk.' At least David and I can
enjoy the long silence while everyone racks their brains
to remember the tiny rewards in their long hours of toil!

But being a fond mother I do attempt to encourage
their finer feelings. And only half-an-hour before I'd
gazed around the table and thought of how each of our
children enriched our lives in such different ways. 'My
best thing,' I smiled, when my turn came round, 'is
being blessed with children who are so brilliant at
cheering me up.' But half-an-hour later as we moved
towards homework I was definitely eating my words.

'I must have left my books on the bus' was mingled
with, 'But you have to let us watch Cliff Richard—he's
only on for an hour, and I'll work twice as hard when
he's over.' Suddenly Lucy blew up as she arranged her

homework on the table. 'John, you horrible boy! Look, he's dropped his wet dishcloth right on the painted shield I'd just finished for history. I'll get shot—but he's the one who ought to be. He always wrecks everything. I can't stand him!' Steffie looked up from scribbling kisses around Miss Adams' hallowed name and reminded Lucy, 'Jesus says you've got to love everybody, so there!' 'No he doesn't,' Lucy grimaced, 'only your neighbour. Not unbearable little brothers. No way!'

But her shrivelling looks just bounced off our un-squashable younger son. I was reminded again what surprises there are in adopting a child, as we'd done with John. It adds all sorts of extra, unexpected flavours to the family genetic stew. John came to live with us when we had three children of our own, and almost from the first, after a traumatic three months, we saw his total buoyancy complementing beautifully our home-grown children's over-sensitivity. That was after this 'I can cope' mother swallowed her pride and, in despera-tion, asked our Christian neighbours to pray for Johnny, and for us. Particularly that he'd begin to respond to the love and discipline meant to help him out of almost constant screaming, and kicking, and scratch-ing people whenever they tried to relate to him. Part of the miracle was his brother's and sisters' continuous battle-scarred love for him. And from the day the prayer began I noticed an increasing peace growing in Johnny, along with his exhibiting the happier side of that unsquashability. And so it has continued. In fact the only time John has spontaneously slumped into absolute submission was when he was totally out for the count. And all due to Great-Aunty Edna. . . .

John had arrived at the lunch table early for once, just

after it had been set by the above-mentioned aunty. She'd carefully placed her bright pink tranquillising pill on the edge of her plate, ready to take with the meal. While Edna continued her knitting in the front room, John, who was alone, discovered an unwanted Smartie just waiting to be eaten. Five minutes later, as the meal began, John's little head slumped heavily into his spaghetti and chips, while Edna wondered whatever she'd done with her pill. And he stayed asleep for two refreshing hours of perfect peace. Or almost perfect peace for us, because we weren't quite sure how John's heart condition might take to being tranquillised.

John had come to us at almost two years old, looking very blue. His colour was due to a bad case of Fallot's tetralogy. That is a serious congenital heart condition, in John's case involving multiple holes in his heart and an almost useless artery from the heart to the lungs. He'd continued to look exceedingly blue for his first few years, causing strangers to stop me in the street and ask if he didn't need wrapping up warmer. So we were very pleased when the hospital decided that, at five years old, he could have grown strong enough for a rather risky operation at the increasingly famous Killingbeck 'heart hospital' in Leeds. He'd be on the waiting list for around six months, we were told.

At about the same time we heard of an evangelistic mission at a small Anglican church over on the other side of Sheffield. The evangelist, Peter Scothern, sees many people healed through his ministry. And somehow the Lord had bells ring for both David and myself that the mission could well bring about healing for John. We both kept hearing from strangers about the mission far too often to be coincidence too, strengthening our conviction that we should be there. (In a large city like Sheffield we could be taking John to healing meetings almost every night of the week. So we had to be sure 'which one'.) Finding that our Bible readings for the day on which we were free to take John to the mission were all about healing, we asked all our friends to pray for a miracle for John that night.

But on the Friday morning before the meeting I answered the phone to hear, 'Good morning, Killingbeck Hospital here.' The surgeon's secretary was giving us the 'wonderful news' that an operation postponement meant John could be admitted the following Monday morning! My heart sank like a stone. However could we tell the hospital that God was showing us to go to a little mission meeting on that day with John instead? So I phoned David at work to see what he thought.

First I explained. Then we prayed together. And then I knew what David was going to say. 'Well, if we're going to continue believing in God's guidance, you'll just have to phone back and explain. And say we'd be very grateful for the next possible date,' David added. We both knew John's heart condition was precarious enough to mean the wait could be fatal—as could the operation. But we both also knew God's guidance to be even more dependable than all our logic.

I picked up the phone, feeling sick at the thought of how the surgeon's secretary would respond to our 'stupidity'. 'Hello, this is John Cook's mother, Sheffield . . .' I began. But suddenly I was interrupted. 'Oh, Mrs Cook, I'm *so* sorry to have raised your hopes like that, but we've just discovered that we've no chance of matching John's blood group for the operation by the beginning of the week. Please forgive our mistake.'

'Well, it might look like a mistake . . .' I said, and then explained to the sympathetic secretary how she was our final sign that John should be over at South Anston on Monday. At the meeting three days later many people went forward for salvation or healing. And so did John. Some people, including his big sister Elinor who was suffering from mesenteric adenitis (complicated tummy-ache), knew they were healed at once. But John just gazed around throughout the laying-on of hands, so that Peter had difficulty in keeping in contact! And then he walked nonchalantly back to his seat, as if he'd just been forward for a better look. But when we returned to the car a little later he ran uphill for the first time ever, beating us all back! And his colour was so improved, we could hardly believe it.

Six months later, the operation showed that he'd somehow grown scores of extra little collateral arteries from his heart to his lungs. And we weren't the slightest bit surprised.

So when the open-heart operation had cleverly bypassed the hopeless pulmonary artery with a Gortex tube, John was *really* pink for a while. Gradually, though, as the tube silted up he became blue again. So even Lucy was relieved that dinner-time, when he woke from his tranquil two hours looking full of beans—even though he'd totally missed his meal!

But strangely enough it was long-suffering Lucy who provided John's best-ever surprise. A surprise that had the neighbours wondering whether he'd received some secret new heart-repair surgery, or something! And so he had, but not in the way they might have thought.

It all began when Lucy, with nothing better to do one Saturday night, decided she'd come with me to a

renewal meeting held nearby in Greenhill Methodist
Church. The building was packed, and as we slipped into
seats at the back of the hall I could sense the joy and
expectancy present among people who were excited to
be worshipping a living Lord Jesus together. And,
presumably, so could Lucy! Because, by the end of the
praise, teaching and testimony, as people were filing
forward for prayer, Lucy was tugging my sleeve
excitedly.

'Mum, why don't you go to the front too,' she
whispered, 'then you could ask the minister to pray for
John?' I gazed at her, amazed at her sudden faith. But as
I smiled my delight at our shy eleven-year-old I realised
that she was the person God wanted to use to channel his
healing to John, not me. And I said so. Poor Lucy looked
horrified at the thought of going forward for prayer with
so many people watching her. And particularly as the
prayer area was high on a very public platform, and
everyone going forward was an adult.

For half a minute she stood undecided. But she knew
John hadn't even been expected by the medical authori-
ties to live beyond five—and he'd been looking much
more blue lately. *What if John doesn't wake up tomorrow
morning? It'll all be my fault*, I could almost hear her
thinking. And suddenly she overcame her shyness and
joined the long queue of people in need.

Twenty minutes later Lucy returned to her seat
looking absolutely radiant. The minister, the Reverend
John Trevenna, had laid his hands on her curly head to
pray by proxy for her little brother, after she'd haltingly
explained his precarious heart condition. But the
blessings that night weren't just for Johnny, because
Lucy, too, received a very special present—and so did we.

For a whole month after that night it was as if Lucy was living in heaven in advance. Nothing was too much trouble, and every day was a delight for her, whatever it seemed like to us. Her big brother and sister must have become pretty sick of having an angel in the house, but the rest of us just basked in the sunshine she radiated around her. And even though Lucy did gradually return to earth, she has been a different daughter ever since that special surprise present. But an even more surprising package was waiting to be opened the next morning!

We were crunching our cornflakes around the breakfast table—all of us except John, who sometimes finds his bed more attractive than breakfast. Then John suddenly made his appearance. He stood on the kitchen step and glared at us. 'I've not had a wink of sleep all night,' he chuntered. 'I've had pins and needles all over me, all night long—in my head, and my legs, and my arms, and my chest and all over!' By now we were all turning to stare at John, still protesting, but amazingly pink. And he kept on grumbling as we flung our arms around him, laughing with delight.

'Johnny, those pins and needles were because Jesus was making your heart and all your blood vessels work even better. He's been healing you some more.' (David and myself, being dental surgeons, know that the only possible cause in John's case for systemic paraesthesia—all over pins and needles—has to be divine intervention, causing blood to flow freely in previously constricted vessels.) And just to prove how God had used Lucy as a channel of his healing power for her little brother, he gave us an extra amazing surprise that afternoon.

We all climbed over the wall opposite our house to

play rounders in the field there with a few little friends. Always until then, despite John's wiry, well-co-ordinated frame, his running limit was first base, where he crouched down on his haunches to pant for a while. But this time John sent the ball flying past the furthest fielder. And as the fielder ran, so did John. Past the first base—smiling past the second base—laughing past the third base—and somersaulting 'home' among the daisies! I guess no one has ever been cheered quite so loud and long.

John's heart still has holes, but tests show that the pulmonary artery is wonderfully healed. So now the holes can start being dealt with. But whether the Lord is going to be working supernaturally, or through surgeons, or both, we know he'll be arranging everything for John to be even more wholehearted in body, soul and spirit! The half-dozen times that God has intervened in miraculous ways in John's young life have already given many opportunities to let the neighbourhood know that Jesus is alive. So with plenty more miracles to look forward to, John's becoming a really brilliant sunshine spreader for the Person who's made it all possible.

In fact, I've sometimes wondered if our children are of more use to their heavenly Father than we are. And especially on the day our three-year-old stopped a train for him! But that's another story.

5

Training for the Race or Racing for the Train?

The most important neighbours we're ever given to love are those we live with. Especially if we've a husband or a wife. They definitely come first in 'loving our neighbour as ourselves'. But however well we're suited, it's always a slow process of learning to put ourselves in the other's place, and it's a skill that takes a lot of practice. (It can be a great blessing to be single, by the way, whether by choice or otherwise, when the Lord is our Managing Director. That way we're free to give and receive so much more care and love in our neighbourhoods than someone committed to the concentrated relationship of marriage.)

Our children come next to our spouses, of course. Because of that fact David and I fast each Saturday to help us hear God's voice for them, and we have a sacrosanct 'family time' for three hours every Tuesday, with the meal and games chosen by each of us in turn.

The area where David and I have had to adapt to each other most is over visitors. And as we're believers who stick closely to the Manufacturer's Handbook when we disagree over anything, it's always in the last resort a case of 'wives, submit yourselves to your husbands' for me—every marriage needing a final court of appeal (Colossians 3:18). David grew up in a family where having a visitor was usually a once-a-year occurrence; but our family was the basically gregarious sort, with visitors there at least once a week for Sunday tea. So when we became Christians, and then realised that surrendering our lives to the Lord included our home being available to him too, we both needed to change our habit patterns to allow visitors to come when he wanted them here, rather than only when it suited us.

Sometimes though a husband and wife can appear so incompatible that divorce seems the only option. And if Jesus weren't able to 'make all things new' David and I would have had to advise divorce more than once for married couples coming for help. But we've seen a number of times now a non-Christian couple meeting Jesus, and their falling in love with him leading them to fall in love with each other again too. And where only one of the couple is a believer and the marriage is coming adrift we've found the prayers and general good-neighbourliness of Christians to both partners has sometimes saved the marriage even before the 'other half' has met the Lord. (Sometimes a bit of wise advice is all that's needed though—like for the zealous, newly-converted husband who was wrecking his marriage through misplaced evangelism for the wife he loved so much. Every time she went to get anything from a drawer, from serviettes to undies, yet another tract would be uncovered, pleading with her to repent and be saved!)

It's well known among Christians now that Satanists are praying against Christian marriages—and probably doubly so where only one partner knows Jesus. But however difficult the trials in Christian or 'mixed marriages' we need to keep on putting our partners first, after Jesus, and then our children next. With God guiding our commitment to all the neighbours he gives too, he will work wonders—as Tina found when her non-Christian husband started to date his secretary, and in her heartbreak she secretly prayed for them both, with the forgiveness that only Christ could enable her to feel. She had to be patient, and very faithful in prayer, because her husband left home and lived with the secretary for a year, leaving her to bring up their three children. But after a year her husband knocked at her door begging her forgiveness and asking if she'd have him back, with an obvious openness to Jesus too. Soon they had a wonderful new marriage to share. It's great that God's 'adapt and survive' instructions can lead on to far more than just surviving!

But we don't usually change overnight, and I've made mistakes; for instance, failing to realise at first that for David one or two visitors a week sharing a meal with us was more than enough. (The many people crowding into our interdenominational prayer-and-praise meetings and Bible studies here on Tuesdays and Thursdays don't affect David as he's at work then.) Gradually, though, more visitors arrived for meals with David's blessing, and sometimes to stay overnight. We trusted the Lord to send the right visitors—the ones we could help, as well as have fun with—and to protect us from those we were no use to. And one of those eminently right visitors was a winner from the start.

'We've got a bootiful princess staying at our house,' breathed starry-eyed young Elinor to anyone willing to listen, that memorable weekend many years ago now. It wasn't just memorable for the company we were keeping, but for the August weather too. The latter was totally, soakingly British, but our royal visitor was obviously not.

Sheela is a cousin of the Nepali royal family, and she came to Britain in order to study for her pharmacy qualifications. During her years here, staying at first with another Sheffield family, she became a much-loved, unofficial aunty to our growing tribe, though a lot of the time she spent studying in distant Liverpool. But her weekend visits to Sheffield were frequent enough to assure our medical friends working in Nepal—who put us in touch in the first place—that Sheela was doing fine.

This particular weekend was totally memorable for Ellie, though, because examinations meant we'd not seen Sheela for months and, being so young, Ellie had forgotten her completely since her last visit. So she was jigging around with joy when Sheela descended from the train looking resplendent in her red and gold sari, and adorned with enough jewels to earn Ellie's forgiveness for forgetting her 'pwincess' cwown'.

She'd not forgotten her capacious umbrella though, which was all to the good because we needed to squash together underneath it as we crossed the now showery station forecourt. And that was the start of that August weekend turning into a record-breaker—for non-stop rain of a totally soaking sort. Our apologies to our Asian guest for such a damp and dismal weekend only resulted in increasingly happy assurances of enjoyment from her, though. Gradually we realised Sheela wasn't just practising her inbuilt Asian politeness—she was actually enjoying getting soaked to the skin every time she ventured out!

'It's true,' she explained, as we sat round the cosy midsummer fire that Saturday evening. 'It is the rain that makes me happy.' And in her still rather stilted English she continued, 'You see, it is in the middle of the three months' monsoon at my home. It is raining—how do you say?—dogs and cats, all the time with my family. But now I can share the monsoon with you—my new family!' And she beamed round at us all.

'Well, as long as you're not praying for three months of it for us too!' I laughed, remembering how really odd weather had accompanied Sheela from her very first visit.

She'd arrived fresh off the plane from Nepal to stay with us while she acclimatised for a few weeks. But she didn't need much acclimatising to the climate, because although it was the middle of autumn she'd brought with her a week's sweltering heatwave! The strangest weather of all, though, materialised months later when Sheela came over from Liverpool for a weekend break from her pharmacology studies.

We decided to take her over the border to a local Derbyshire beauty spot for a picnic, as the sun began to blaze that June morning. 'How are you going to sun-bathe in your sari?' young Matthew asked Aunty Sheela, as he raced off to the swimsuit cupboard, followed at a fast crawl by his little sister. I explained to Sheela that the dale we were visiting is dissected by a perfect stream for paddling and dam-building, plus sunbathing on the side for me. 'Don't worry, Aunty Sheela,' added Matthew, dashing back with the cricket bat too. 'You're brown enough already. You can play cricket with me instead.'

Half an hour later, as we drove to our destination we

could hardly believe our eyes. Floating in front of them were soft, solitary flakes of snow! And before very long a thick curtain of it. So, by the time we arrived, there was a white carpet stretching as far as the eye could see. Only a thin carpet, mind you, because the snowfall soon stopped. But it was thick enough to make sunbathing seem a bit silly when the June sun emerged briefly again ten minutes later, cheering our chilly repast as we huddled by the car.

That weekend was memorable for more than the weather, though, because the house almost burst at the seams on the Sunday as all sorts of friends and relatives and their families 'just happened' to call, in passing. Our house had never seemed quite so much like a transport café, especially by Sunday tea-time when we ran out of cups. We might have indulged in the ancient Yorkshire custom of sipping tea out of saucers instead, except a neighbour came round with an emergency supply—and the rest of her family too! They were followed by my sister Jane and her entertaining husband and children, with delicious home-made cakes. (We really should swop surnames!)

So Sheela found herself with plenty of engrossing conversation practice that particular Sunday. So much so that she suddenly realised she'd forgotten the time, and should have left for the train back to Liverpool five minutes before.

'Excuse us everybody,' I interrupted, 'I'll be home again soon.' David had already left the party because he was booked to preach at a nearby church that evening. I bundled Matthew into the car with us, and as we dashed to the station I prayed aloud for Sheela, in the panic of knowing there wasn't another train back to Liverpool that night. I don't know whether Sheela was praying, as she's basically Hindu, but I said, 'Thank you, Lord Jesus, that you can hold up the train if necessary till Sheela arrives. And you'll help me drive as safely and as speedily as possible. And please could you save us a parking space?' 'Amen' chorused Matthew, used to being a back-seat prayer partner!

As we arrived at the station we smiled to see the car nearest the entrance drive away from its parking space in perfect synchronisation with us. Sheela raced to the thankfully empty ticket office with sari in full sail, while we lugged her book-heavy suitcase to the barrier. 'Platform 7, I'm afraid,' smiled the ticket collector wryly. 'You'll have to run.' And so we did, our pounding feet echoing across the wooden bridge to the top of the steps leading to the very last platform . . . where we stopped in our tracks. There was the Liverpool train slowly starting to glide out of the station.

'Oh no!' Sheela and I gasped breathlessly at each other. But Matthew didn't. He shot down that long flight of clattery wooden steps as fast as his fat little legs would carry him. And he shouted at the top of his voice as he went, an ear-splitting, 'Wait for Aunty Sheela!'

As we stared at the disappearing train the guard stuck his head out of the window, glanced at young Matthew . . . and slowly the train ground to a halt. 'Come on, Aunty Sheela,' called the self-possessed train-stopper. 'They're waiting for you.' And as Sheela and I speedily hugged each other goodbye in a state of happy shock, matter-of-fact Matthew waved to the guard with the air of someone who knows that of course trains will stop, if only you shout loud enough!

Actually, Matthew taught me a lot. Not only that I

could at last rejoice over passing on my antecedents' raucous vocal-cords to our infants, but also that God often wants us to be part of the answers to our own prayers. And that we must keep on expecting and acting on those answers till the very last minute—which is often later than we in our mature wisdom think it could be. And lastly, to be so single-minded in seeing God's purposes work out that we don't care what anyone else, neighbours or not, think about us. Especially when what he thinks is so much more important.

But of course I've sometimes slipped back into 'What will the neighbours say?' type responses since then, when I should have known better. Especially when visitors to our house have been less than like-minded. The saddest time was when a rather formal church-going family were with us for tea. I could quickly tell they'd already decided we were over the top with our Christian sticker on the door, and with our talk about Jesus as if he might walk in at any moment.

Suddenly, though, someone else did walk in—and he was slightly reminiscent of popular pictures of Jesus, too. A tall young man with dark curly hair and a beard, and even wearing Jesus sandals! Our mutual friend Margaret had brought Chris round to meet us, obviously concerned for him. He was very much alone in the world, and had been receiving treatment for acute depression. Margaret is very skilful at helping people in mental and emotional distress, having experienced plenty herself, and she managed to signal to me that Chris, despite his calm exterior, still needed plenty of help that afternoon.

He must have been a great actor, though, because he managed to appear chatty and almost outgoing. And so

the thought I'd had that perhaps we should ask Chris
whether he'd like us to pray with him, even though he
wasn't a believer, was pushed to the back of my mind.
This was partly because I didn't want to embarrass him,
but mainly because I didn't want our guests to think I
was addicted to being superspiritual, even though I had
the perfect opportunity to ask Chris as we all enjoyed tea
together. . . .

Generally we give thanks for meals as we finish
them—that way we're usually all present, even if extra-
curricular activities cause any of us to be late in arriving
for the feast. And also we can really mean our thanks
(usually!) for the meal we've just received. Sometimes
the giving-thanks can turn into a general prayer time for
anyone whose needs have surfaced during the meal. So
everything was set up for us to pray for Chris together.
But I wondered again what our daunting guests would
think of such embarrassing fanaticism—particularly if
God brought supernatural gifts like discernment of the
root causes of Chris' depression to bear. So I pushed the
idea totally out of my mind. The next day we were
devastated to hear that Chris had hanged himself. Who
knows, the prayer together might have made all the
difference.

It was a comfort, though, to know that suicide *isn't* the
unforgiveable sin (Luke 12:10 and Hebrews 6:4–6), and
that Chris could even have become a secret believer
through Margaret's caring prayer and help, in spite of
Satan managing to convince him for that moment that
suicide was the only way out. But the fact that we'd
failed this neighbour the Lord had sent us made me
learn a hard but useful lesson. So now remembering
poor Chris helps to set me free from the trap of being

imprisoned by other people's opinions where matters of life and death, or even what seem like totally insignificant trivia, are concerned. And whether we're racing for a train or trying to save a life, we need to keep on training for the race and forcing ourselves on—because the rewards really are too mindblowing to miss.

6

Water into . . ?

Nowadays we've finally discovered the perfect family devotions slot. Perfect for us, that is. Which doesn't necessarily mean it's any use at all to any other family. But after years of trying every timetable imaginable for fitting in some family prayer and praise every day—manoeuvring around Cubs, dancing classes, school buses and work delays, plus being interrupted by telephone calls, toilet calls, friends to play and milkmen to pay—we've finally cracked it!

So the only interruptions now are either from our elderly and lonely flat-dwelling friend, Richard, who's an inveterate early riser and can't stay in, or from my elderly, loving mum who's on the phone but not in the best of health and can't get out. Our new routine has the Jesus-time happening every morning at 7.15 am—I wish I could say 'on the dot', but I defy any family with five children to start anything to the second. Especially when they are all needing the bathroom at once!

The only worry I have is that as the children leave home they'll find themselves totally unable to rise from their beds without the life-transfusing tea their mother kindly wakes them with every morning. As most Yorkshire folk know, the minimal amount of caffeine in tea is just what you need, when getting up in the morning feels like rising from the dead—as well, of course, as a mother who's trained herself to rise a good deal earlier, without any artificial stimulant at all!

But at least the system means we're all down and dressed, ready to praise the Lord at the very beginning of our day—and if Richard's joining in too it just makes the Jesus-time richer. Especially since Richard, at nearly eighty, has spent a lifetime in the pub, when he's not been down the coal mine, and had never been near a church until a year ago. I had suddenly thought to ask the unkempt, weary-looking gentleman waiting for a bus at the bottom of our very long, steep road whether he'd like a lift. He was breathing like a grampus due to chronic bronchitis and a bad heart, so he was really grateful to escape the cold air. It turned out he had recently moved into the neighbouring bedsits, ten houses up from us. When I asked him to tea and a fellowship meeting at our house a few lifts later, he accepted with alacrity.

It was the meal, of course, rather than the fellowship, that attracted him. But Richard stayed to the meeting and found himself introduced to all sorts of new friends. Friends whose hugging of all and sundry wasn't influenced—well, not much anyway—by paltry matters like a lack of personal hygiene, and who obviously were delighted to meet him. But there was one very important introduction he made all by himself. Because, as he slowly walked back up to his bedsit that night, he kept thinking of the joy on our faces as we'd worshipped the Lord—and he knew that joy was what he'd secretly been seeking all his life.

So, for the first time since he'd knelt to pray as a five-year-old to please his mum, he knelt at the side of his bed and said, 'Jesus, I don't know if I'm much use to ya, but I want to be yours like they are. Thank you fer dyin' fer me and me sins. Now I want ta live fer you.' And three months later Richard was baptised by full immersion. 'Foolishness, with your bad chest!' warned a neighbour. But for Richard, making his stand for Christ in the waters of baptism seemed to bless his body and soul, as well as his spirit. So we look forward to his Jesus-time calls for years to come!

But Richard wasn't the first Jesus-time drop-in to experience a watery blessing. Ten-year-old Jane happened to call to play with Elinor one day when we were still in that period of fighting a losing battle with the old post-dinner-time slot for praising the Lord, around the cleared dining table. Dessert was still underway when Jane arrived, so she stood warming herself against the dining-room radiator while she waited, that cold autumn day.

As we swung into the Jesus-time with a song, I beckoned to Jane to join us. Hopefully she'd find some inner warmth, too, though praise meetings weren't her usual scene. She sat herself down happily enough between Elinor and little Lucy, as Matthew read the Bible passage. 'Right now, everyone, eyes closed,' ordered David, as a discussion ensued about whether walking on the water would be faster than swimming through it. I don't remember who was imminently going where that night, but someone was bound to be going somewhere in a hurry! So we closed our eyes for some speedy prayers. Eyes closed to pray around the table at our house always means hands together too. Not in front of us, though, but person-to-person. Linking hands in a circle with everyone reminds us that in the circle of God's love even the youngest member is a vital link in receiving and giving. And any visitors, like Jane, are immediately able to feel at home and one of the family in this sometimes sticky-fingered celebration of being all one in Christ Jesus.

A second or two later we were all praying out loud, one by one, as is the rule in our house—whether we feel like it or not (except for visitors of course who have a special dispensation!). We want to communicate 'be ye constant in prayer' to the children by example, from the earliest possible age. And we often need reminding that, even if we don't feel like praying, God always feels like answering our prayers—according to our 'need and not our greed', as the children have discovered. So as the prayers criss-crossed around the table that tea-time I hoped Jane would become aware of God's presence too. And suddenly I sensed in my spirit that the reason Jane was with us was because God wanted her to discover his healing power for herself, through a need she'd had now for a year or two; and that our prayer together would set that discovery in motion.

'Please, Lord Jesus,' Jane heard me pray a few seconds later, 'will you heal Jane's cystitis, and bless her and her family all very much indeed.' Since the cystitis hadn't been helped by the usual medication, Jane's doctor had referred her to the hospital and now she was taking long-term medication for a year, in the hope of a cure. But suddenly I felt certain her treatment was being taken over by Dr Jesus, and it was happening in the twinkling of an eye instead.

Just as I arrived at the 'Amen' there was an echoing

watery crash! So of course we all opened our eyes and
stared at an astonishing sight. Little Lucy had contrived,
with her hand in Jane's, to knock over her glass of water.
There was nothing strange about that; she was always
doing it. But the shape the spilled water had assumed
totally took our breath away. It had formed an absolutely perfect fish! The cork-topped table displayed the
fishy shape to perfection, and the water had so spilled
that the fish was centrally placed right in front of Jane,
staring up at her. This miraculous fish even had a
perfectly formed eye, due to a little circle where the
water hadn't quite met across the cork, and it was in
exactly the place where a fish's eye should be situated!
There were fins and a tail in all the right places too.
And, even more staggering, there wasn't one extraneous
drop of water left over from Lucy's clumsy accident—
every last drop was part of the perfectly placed fish.

Well, we all knew what the fish was doing there—a
literal fish out of water! It had to be our heavenly Father
saying 'Amen' to that prayer for Jane that he'd given me
to pray. And he was encouraging our family at the same
time too, because just that week we'd all been learning
about the Ichthus sign. All except Jane, of course. So
between us we explained to her about *ichthus*, the Greek
word for fish, on a handy piece of notepaper.

	I		JESUS
(The first	CH	standing	CHRIST
letters of the	TH		GOD'S
Greek words)	U	for	SON
	S		SAVIOUR

Then we told Jane how the fish shape became the secret
sign of the early, persecuted Christians, pointing like an

arrow drawn on the dusty paths—nose first—to all their rendezvous, and secret meetings. 'And if you look on my jacket, Jane, you'll see a little gilt fish there. It helps as a conversation starter to tell other people a bit about Jesus, and also for me to meet other Christians who know the fish sign too, because we can introduce ourselves when we see it.' Then suddenly I remembered how this conversation had come about, and smiled across at our young friend.

'Jane, I wouldn't be surprised if your miracle fish is a special sign from God for you to say you're not going to be bothered by cystitis again,' I added, as Jane stared at me, 'because God sometimes does in a split-second what it can take a hospital a whole year to sort out.' Suddenly Jane's eyes shone with anticipation as seeing became believing for her. But, of course, she had to keep taking the tablets until the end of the year, so it wasn't a miracle that witnessed to anyone other than ourselves. It was a special family-time miracle that will live in our hearts all our lives, as we remember the day Jesus turned water into a fish for the sake of someone he loves very much.

And it was a miracle of healing that Jane was well-prepared for too! Because all the children's friends, right from playing here as toddlers, were used to hearing David and myself, as well as our offspring, interrupt any activity, as a problem arose, with prayer. 'Arrow' prayers, shot up to the Father who expects us to send our needs to him immediately they materialise—in normal day-to-day English, too—over anything from hurt feelings, to lost keys, to a broken leg!

So I'd sometimes find an agnostic mum or dad telling me how their offspring, after playing at our house, had said something like, 'Please, Jesus, make our car go,'

when the ignition wouldn't work, and suddenly it had
sprung into life! All useful pre-evangelism among a
sceptical population. 'They even pray on the phone at
Ellie's house, Mum,' one of Ellie's playmates reported
when she arrived back home. 'And it must work because
a little girl who was nearly dead, on one of those
machines in hospital that keep you breathing when you
can't, suddenly started to breathe again just at the time
when they prayed with her grandma on the phone!' A
useful reminder of how our homes can be one of the
most potent mission-fields. Especially when they're fre-
quented by people like my friend Barbara, healed of
both cancer and severe arthritis in the few short years
since she met Jesus, and brilliantly aglow with him.

Sometimes we've seen miracles in the family circle that
have meant healing not for an outsider, but for one of
the members. For instance, my first book, *What Will the
Neighbours Say?* recounts how God used our three-year-
old as a power channel for his little sister. And as we're
all children of the world's leading Consultant in every
medical field, our first response when anyone in the
family is afflicted, by any ailment at all, has to be asking
for his opinion—and his treatment too. If we still need
medical aid (or dental treatment!) after that, then we'll
seek it, but often we find we don't.

God's healing sometimes comes into the family along
anonymous channels, because plenty of people are
praying for us at a distance as we are for them. (Particularly we pray for missionary families, and Christians and
others undergoing persecution and suffering around
the world.) And most of all, our prayer support comes
from our natural family, spread around Britain and
further afield, like David's sister Ruth and family in

Australia, and the many brothers and sisters God has given us here too.

We've occasionally heard from someone that they just had a 'hunch' they should pray for us when they hadn't a clue about our needs at the time. That's happened more than once with my elder brother, Peter, praying over in Dublin with his faith-filled wife, Joan, and their four children. Peter came to Christ in his forties and immediately became a very obedient believer—especially in the area of living very simply so that others, in the third world, might simply live. And his compassionate care for all his nearby neighbours as well as the far-flung and family neighbours God gave him, meant ever-increasing answers to prayer.

The most memorable occasion was through Peter attending a meeting in Dublin where the visiting speaker was an American Catholic priest with a special ministry for hearts. Physical hearts, that is. Peter had seen the meeting advertised on a Catholic poster as he travelled around the city in his work as a civil engineer. Immediately he thought of our young Peter John with his heart condition. He was named Peter after my elder brother, and John after my younger brother—another very caring uncle who, with his lovely wife and family, now lives down in Plymouth. The second name, John, was the one that stuck, though, because our new little adopted son was called John when he arrived here. (The foster mother who'd looked after him for a week, between his first eighteen months spent in hospital and his coming to us, disliked his original Christian name intensely. It was Wayne, and she couldn't bring herself to use it at all. But she did like John Wayne, the film star, so little Wayne was answering to John already by the time he reached us!)

Anyway, as my brother Peter perused the poster on the train, he realised the meeting was at a time he'd be free. And that even though little John was across the Irish sea in Sheffield, God could channel his healing, with distance no obstacle, through Peter receiving the laying-on of hands in John's place. So, a few days later, he was sitting in a Dublin auditorium, enjoying the American priest's Bible-centred exposition of healing. There were so many people there needing prayer for body, soul and spirit after the talk that Peter had plenty of time to pray for John himself, and for the people around him too in the long queue of needs. But finally he was able to receive prayer himself for that distant damaged heart. And he was surprised, in the great spirit of expectancy present there, to feel none of the power and peace that can accompany the laying-on of hands. In fact he felt nothing at all.

Nothing, that is, until he was halfway back to his seat. Suddenly, as he climbed the steps, he had to lean against the wall, gripped by a terrible pain in his chest. Peter had never experienced any heart trouble at all, but he was sure that he must be suffering a really bad heart attack. And maybe a terminal one. . . .

'But, Lord,' he gasped inwardly, 'I can't leave Joan and the children on their own!' 'Don't you think I can look after them better than you can?' the Lord answered. And in the couple of seconds that that thought-conversation lasted, Peter suddenly received a tremendous peace, and a tremendous expectation too—he was sure he was going to see the Lord face to face at any moment! Then, just as quickly as it came, the pain totally disappeared, leaving Peter almost disappointed for a split second, but then so thrilled at the thought of staying with the precious family he'd just surrendered so absolutely to his loving Lord.

It wasn't until the next morning, as he awoke, that Peter suddenly realised the possible significance of his psuedo heart attack. 'Maybe it was something to do with the reason for the prayer,' he thought, 'God giving John a new heart in exchange for his congenitally-damaged old one.' So he reached for pen and paper (writing always coming more naturally to him than telephoning) and related to us the events of the previous evening. He finished by asking us to double-check John's condition, 'just in case'.

Glancing across the breakfast table three days later as I read the letter confirmed my impression that John's rather dusky skin hadn't become any pinker lately. But then David began to read the letter and looked very thoughtful. 'Peter says the meeting was on Wednesday night,' he noticed, out loud. 'Well, that's very interesting. I'd not liked to tell you, love, but increasingly lately I've kept feeling twinges in my chest almost daily over the last few weeks.' I stared at my squash-playing husband in horror. He'd recently performed a parachute jump for charity, and the doctor had found him to be in good health. But being on the wrong side of forty, I knew anything could happen. His otherwise very fit mother had suddenly died one tragic night of a totally unexpected heart attack, when not so much older than David is now. And he certainly took after his mother's side of the family.

'But you can stop looking so worried,' smiled my dear undeparted. 'Since Wednesday I've been feeling totally fit, without one sign of trouble. I guess the Lord has used Peter as a wonderfully powerful channel of healing. Only it wasn't for John, it was for me!'

Well, I don't know who was the most surprised by God's mystery miracle—David, myself, or Peter (when we telephoned him later that day). But I know I've continued to be more grateful to Peter than words can say, and even more so to God, that John and his brother and sisters have a wonderfully fit father. An athletic, still squash-playing, rough-and-tumbling dad, whose heart couldn't behave better.

One of the impossible-to-understand mysteries that our family, and far more importantly, Joan and Peter's family, have to live with, is that two years ago, without warning, Peter did go to be with the Lord after all. It happened during a sudden asthma attack at home one night, leaving Mary, Joseph, John and little James, to share with their mum, and all our wider family, their heartbreaking loss. But also to share with everyone their uplifting faith and selflessness. And particularly so in Joan's ministry through returning to her pre-motherhood role as a very gifted health visitor, while blessing her children more than many couples manage together.

And Peter is a brilliant reminder to us that, as long as we're channels of God's love, he'll always direct his love in exactly the right way. It can sometimes be in a different direction from the one we expected, and can often produce a different result. But our wonder-working Father will always bless his children in just the way we need if we're willing to love each other with his love. That means his love for the family we so often take for granted. For the family of God around us too. And for the whole family of man, as God shows us how—his way.

WORK-OUT 2
Neighbours in the Family

Helping every feeble neighbour—seeking help from none
(Adam Gordon, 1833–70)

Neighbours are what you get when a horse meets
a bee—neigh-buzz (get it?!)—and sometimes
the bee might sting!
(Stephanie Cook, 1983–)

1. HOME IS WHERE THE HEART IS
Families need to be fed on a diet of love and discipline,
with large helpings of forgiveness.
Read 2 Corinthians 2:7 and Mark 11:25.

(a) What is the right balance for our children between
having fun and obeying the rules? How can we
motivate our children into loving their neighbours?
(b) Why is forgiveness often more costly among
families—and also more powerful? Is there anyone
you can't forgive?
(c) Does the honesty usually inherent in families help or
hinder the growth of love?
(d) How could our homes be more useful to the Lord?
Is the second half of Gordon's sentiment (above)
ever right?

2. TRAINING FOR THE RACE OR RACING FOR THE TRAIN?
As the twenty-first century approaches we live in an
increasingly multi-cultural mission-field.
Read Ephesians 2:1–10 and Hebrews 13:1–2.

(a) In what ways is Christianity unique among the other world faiths?

(b) How might persecution result from evangelism among other faiths in this country, the Christian's proclamation of John 14:6 (that Jesus is the only way to God), and the inability of evangelicals to join in multi-faith services and movements?

(c) Could you entertain or befriend a lonely overseas student? How should you go about it?

(d) Is it a bad witness to people of other faiths and none to pray about such trivial details as finding a parking space?

3. WATER INTO . . . ?
Read Mark 10:13–16.

(a) How best can we teach our children to pray through the day (not just at night, when we pray with them)?

(b) What lower age limit would one set for the gifts of the Spirit, such as healing and speaking in tongues, to operate through children?

(c) An increasing number of families experience the trauma of wife-battering, alcohol addiction and child abuse. Can divorce ever be justified for a Christian in such situations? (See Mark 10:2–12.) How can we help victims, children or adults, to forgive but to be safeguarded from further attacks?

(d) How should our faith and surrender to Christ affect our lifestyle—eg, our spending on food, compared with our giving to the third world, or our spending on our homes compared with spending on our churches?

Praise Point: 'Go back home to your family and tell them how much the Lord has done for you' (Mark 5:19).

PART THREE
Neighbours at Work

7

Working Flat Out

Arriving at work on time, as any working mother knows, is often more difficult for her than for the average working father. Just about everyone, from children who've lost a shoe to phone callers with 'important' messages, seems to imagine that Mum is somehow more able to work time-stretching miracles—or that punctuality doesn't matter quite as much for her as for Dad!

Actually, we haven't suffered from 'lost shoe' lateness for years, ever since we started the strict rule that shoes stay together on the stairs the second they are separated from feet! The shoes are tucked tidily out of the sight of visitors entering through the front door, in case they think with all that footwear we've a shoe repair business on the side! Because our real 'family business'—of caring for people in an area with many needy neighbours—certainly causes plenty of people to call at our door.

So, with the struggle it takes for me to make it through the front door in the opposite direction, it often seems that my part-time work, once I arrive, is a total rest-cure. That was the way it was looking one bright spring morning a while ago, as I strolled through the city centre on my way to our practice, thinking how blessed I was to be a dentist. Not only do I generally have to cope with only one person's needs at a time (unlike at home where crises usually arrive in droves), but I have a dental nurse to protect me from unnecessary interruptions, and to synchronise my timetable for me.

On top of that, dentistry gives the tremendous satisfaction of many disciplines in one, as I'd been explaining to a questioning friend who'd wondered why anyone would want to 'look down in the mouth' all day long! With my first dental practice having a principal who was both a doctor and a dentist, but who chose to practise dentistry because he'd discovered more satisfaction in dealing with the world's most common disease, I knew I was in the right job from the start. Dentists probably do know more practical fulfilment than most professional people, even though a fair amount of time *is* spent in sculpturing fillings—an art form in itself! There is lots of aesthetic satisfaction too in moving crooked teeth into pleasing symmetry, and remodelling sunken smiles with face-saving dentures. Then there's the satisfaction, for everyone concerned, of extracting the causes of excruciating pain, plus prescribing miracle-working drugs for all sorts of mouth pathologies. And we can practise being radiographers and anaesthetists too, as necessary. And there are sometimes minor surgical operations to be performed as well. It never fails to put me in my place, as I'm stitching up after a spot of oral surgery, that however well any medical worker operates we're all totally stuck unless the healing power that God has placed in human bodies then takes over. Those stitches could stay there for a year, and still be all that's holding two separate surfaces together, without the body's brilliant repair mechanism taking over to close the gap.

'What about the poor patient, though, while you're enjoying all that job satisfaction?' you might be wondering. Well, the patient's fine, because what I enjoy perhaps most of all is practising the psychology that enables petrified patients to turn into relaxed friends, knowing they really do have nothing to fear. So, as I drew near the surgery door that fine spring morning, I found that counting my blessings had me well psyched-up for a fulfilling four hours of work. But I suddenly remembered that my watch was five minutes slow—and that my first patient was a terribly talkative lady coming for new dentures. And I dashed into the practice so fast that I nearly missed a very strange sight.

There, behind the anaesthetic machine in the corner of the first surgery, was the prone figure of my partner. He was flat on his back on the floor, with no nurse to be seen. 'Whatever's he doing?' I questioned myself in mid-flight. 'Maybe he's running out of angles to view the gas machine's inner workings, because they're not! Or perhaps he's been secretly addicted to nitrous oxide all this time, and the poor nurse has found him overdoing it and fled!' Either way, I knew I'd better let any impatient patients know they'd soon be seen, by hurrying into my surgery and sitting 'Mrs Garrulous' in the chair to entertain the nurse. And then I nipped back to check Mike's state of health after his start-of-the-session slip—of whatever sort!

As I whizzed into his surgery again I wasn't any the wiser—he was still prone, but the nurse was back and filling in forms. 'Is it a new method of meditation he's trying before the day's work begins?' I wondered. 'And the nurse just takes it in her stride now? At least she wouldn't have to stride over him *too* often, lying neatly behind the gas machine like that!'

Suddenly my meandering thoughts were interrupted. 'Hello, Hilary,' said Mike, seeing me moving tentatively towards him. 'I'm stuck down here because I was just putting a new gas cylinder on the machine when my back gave way. It's my old disc trouble, and I'm just gently trying to get myself together enough to get up again. I'm afraid I'll have to go home.'

Oh no, I thought. *Then I'll have to squeeze Mike's patients into my heavy schedule too.* 'It'll all work out, I'm sure,' was what I said, though. 'Can I help you get upright?'

'No, thanks,' Mike grimaced. 'I'll have to do it very gradually.'

Although he wasn't a believer, he knew I was, so as I dashed back to my denture lady I added, 'I'll be praying for you.' It was encouraging to hear Mike say, 'Thank you,' instead of, 'A fat lot of good that'll do.' He was probably thinking the latter, as a scientific humanist, but pain can have a way of broadening our options.

A second later I had my options broadened too. As I darted back through the waiting room to my surgery, I suddenly noticed a couple from the local house church, arrived early for an appointment with me. Peter had come to hold his wife Helen's very nervous hand on this first visit to our practice. And as I smiled a welcome to them, an idea came into my head that, carried out, could mean this would be their last visit too. But it wouldn't be anything to do with my dentistry—just my impertinence! I was wondering whether they would be willing to pray with me for Mike—not in my surgery, when their turn came for treatment, but straight away, back in Mike's surgery, where we could lay hands on him together in a New Testament way, to pray for his healing—if he was willing.

Peter and Helen smiled back at me expectantly as I went over to them. But their smiles turned to surprise, then apprehension, as I took them into my surgery to explain. (At least there were only a couple of pairs of listening ears there, instead of a waiting room full—even our loquacious first lady managing to draw breath long enough to discover the reason for the invasion.) As Helen and Peter realised the pain Mike was in—and the length of time everyone would be waiting for treatment, short of a miracle—they nervously agreed to join me in asking the Lord to raise the dentist.

And raising the dead seemed only slightly more difficult, as we trooped in together a minute later, after Mike had given an I'll-try-anything-once OK to my embarrassing suggestion. Peter took his courage in both hands and placed them on Mike's horizontal shoulders as we crouched around him, wondering what the dental nurse thought of our unusual treatment methods.

'Please, Father, touch our brother's back and heal him, for your glory and his blessing. Thank you, Lord, Amen.' Peter's surgically to-the-point prayer said it all. And the only surprise before we hurried out of the surgery, without waiting to see whether Mike leapt to his feet—in case he didn't—was the heartwarming sound of not just three 'Amens' or even four, but a full complement of five! Secretly I was thinking, with my faith only just mustard-seed size, that any other miracle was very unlikely, with our obvious lack of fire and fervour.

Especially as I'd only set the prayer session in motion out of obedience to what the Bible says should be the Christian's reaction in such situations, not because of any surge of faith for Mike's healing.

So a minute later, when I discovered I needed some more wax from Mike's surgery for my now silenced denture patient, I was glad I could send the nurse for it. Or could I? The chorus we'd sung in our family Jesus-time that morning suddenly made a come-back into my cowardly mind. 'Be bold, be strong . . .' was definitely not what I wanted to remember at that moment, but I could hardly ignore it after encouraging our children to live it out that morning. So, with a rueful smile at Peter and Helen as I passed through the waiting room yet again, I set about silently praising the Lord for whatever I was going to find. And though I knew very well that I should leave with God the consequences of what he sets in motion, I still had that sinking feeling as I opened Mike's door and forced myself to look in his direction.

But a second later I was blurting out, 'I don't believe it!' Because I glanced at where Mike had been lying and saw only his feet, with the rest of him bending over his first patient! He gave me a confident thumbs up sign and a meaningful look as he told me, 'I think it's more than my back that's been restored.' As I beamed back at him with an involuntary 'Praise the Lord!' it didn't seem to matter that the nurse and maybe the waiting room could hear me. And as Helen and Peter kept their happy secret to themselves out there, they realised that Helen was no longer desperate to run in the wrong direction either, and could really trust the Lord about her teeth. As so often happens, praying for a neighbour in need had put her own need into perspective. And we had all been wonderfully reminded that God is the God of miracles.

Helen's miracle, to my mind, was as amazing as Mike's. She was one of the surprisingly large number of adult Christians for whom dental treatment is a nightmare. The Lord's instructions to 'fear not' were for her impossible to apply to dentistry, along with many other 'decaying' saints! But at least Helen forced herself as far as the dental waiting room unlike many of her fellow-sufferers who daren't, despite their faith. That old joke about a very nervous mother sitting in the dental chair for fillings is grounded in oft-repeated reality:

Patient: 'Oh dear, I'm so nervous, I think I'd rather have a baby than a filling.'

Dentist: 'Well please make up your mind so I can adjust the chair accordingly.'

But Helen had been gloriously set free from such paralysing fear. In fact it wasn't long before visiting the surgery was almost a pleasure!

However, it wasn't only Helen who, in the days ahead, discovered that he will sometimes apply his wonder-working power even to teeth when we ask him . . .

8
Cliff-Hanging Celebration

It has always been my experience that a noisy waiting room is one of the dentist's most important assets. The paralysing fear that can grip us—the generation of the pre-fluoride era—while waiting to sit on that 'electric chair', is often wonderfully defused by an entertaining fellow-patient with enough 'gift of the gab' to take our mind off our molars. Or walls that (due to the generosity of our local infant school) are plastered with children's illustrations of dentists extracting massive gnashers from pin-men patients, and the like—the product of different classes 'doing teeth'. Sometimes the junior school may make a contribution too, for example, this delightful doggerel on a colleague's wall:

> You must not bite your dentist
> When she looks inside your head.
> Your dentist is your teeth's best friend;
> Bite someone else instead!

Television can be another useful tranquilliser in the waiting room, especially when it's showing *Neighbours* or

Playbus or the Test Match, depending on the patients—though sometimes pin-striped businessmen can get so lost in *Playbus* and they are lulled into such a womb-like security that they don't even hear their names called! And dental videos can do wonders in motivating patients to put their teeth back in (I don't mean their dentures) the priority slot they deserve.

But probably one of my best assets in calming patients over the years has been our offspring as they've arrived on the scene. While Grandma's been looking after the current pre-schooler for my two or three sessions of dentistry a week, I've often taken the breast-feeding baby with me to work (with appointment book suitably punctuated), or the toddler when Grandma's been otherwise occupied. And their therapeutic effect on the waiting room has been priceless. As soon as the infant has grown old enough to enjoy relating to the patients, he or she has had a great time sitting on sometimes the most unlikely knees, being read to, or sung to, or helped with a jigsaw. And as the patients realise by the process of elimination that the happy little child must belong to the dentist, it does wonders for their confidence in my not being the ogre I might have seemed.

But the prize for producing our must useful waiting room diversion ever must go to Rachel. She was the new dental nurse who, in the end, found dentistry a bit beyond her, but who excelled at exuding confidence and charm. And even in persuading patients they were going to have a wonderful time when they passed that surgery door! Her great love in life was Cliff Richard and, if she'd had her way, the waiting room would have been covered with wall hangings of her hero. And if I'd only known what a cliff-hanger I was going to experience one unexpected day because of the man himself appearing in Sheffield in person, I'd have taken Rachel with me, to charm her way through the crowds to his hallowed side!

Instead, however, the Lord had me learn one or two useful lessons through doing it the hard way—getting to him, I mean, to interview him for Radio Sheffield's religious programme. For years now I've been producing a five-minute interview each week for our local radio station's Sunday output—and enjoying the discovery that a shared experience of a living Lord, whether from street cleaners or TV stars, can have far more life-changing impact than even the most engrossing theological debate.

Like the day that Mary, a pensioner belonging to our church, and unaware of the Christian radio programme, switched on for the news too early and heard my voice as I interviewed international evangelist Reinhard Bonnke. So she kept listening. A minute later I asked Reinhard to pray for any listeners who were ill. Mary had terminal cancer, but as Reinhard prayed she felt the power of God go through her body and her healing had begun.

So, when I heard that Cliff was in one of the central bookshops in Sheffield signing copies of his latest book, I was soon ready to set off with my recording equipment.

However, I'd only heard about the event one hour before it began, and I had no chance to pre-arrange an interview, even if Cliff were willing and able to grant me one. But the thought of Kate, our neighbour down the road, spurred me on to try. Kate was a trendy left-wing atheist who was convinced that Cliff was a hypocrite, amassing himself a fortune under an assumed religious disguise. Knowing the truth through our involvement with Tear Fund (the charity which for years has channelled the proceeds from his nationwide concert tours to third world relief), I longed to interview him as the devil's advocate. Then all the 'Kates' in our listening area could hear Cliff setting the record straight on his personal faith and commitment.

When I realised the bookshop holding his 'sign-in' was only two minutes away from our surgery, and that he'd be signing books for the hour before I began work that day, I knew I must be meant to go along and try to catch Cliff. The only trouble was that trying turned out to be very trying! The massed crowds outside—and then inside—the shop made my progress very slow. And as I struggled up the stairs to the first floor 'sign-in' spot, I found a hefty employee posted at the top of them. He was just managing to hold his own amid the surging masses as he told me there wasn't a hope of interviewing Cliff, even if I managed to reach him—his schedule was far too tight to include the press.

But there was still almost half an hour to go before work so, with childhood memories of my father's 'nothing ventured, nothing gained' echoing in my ears, I ploughed forward. A few minutes later, by dint of holding the microphone high enough for people to see I might be about important business, I managed to catch a glimpse of Cliff. He was seated at the centre of a very long table behind a stack of hundreds of his paperbacks, and with a couple of 'bodyguards' for good measure. At one end of the table hovered a short, fat, cheerful-looking character, and he was balanced by a tall, thin, rather miserable-looking man at the other. The massed humanity was gradually attaining its goal of Cliff's coveted signature on the slowly shrinking piles of paperbacks. But with twenty minutes to go before work I needed to act quickly.

'Which end should I try, Lord?' I whispered inwardly, but really it was a silly prayer. So I used my common sense and pushed through to the short gentleman as politely as I could. I felt very embarrassed, arriving at his side, to realise that suddenly almost every eye was on the diversion of me and my mike. *I'm going to look such a fool if he says 'no' in front of all these people*, I thought. *I hope there's no one here that I know.* But the stakes seemed worth it. Especially, I reminded myself, with the Lord's hall-mark of his timing on the whole thing. If I'd known, however, that my dental nurse was there in the middle of that mass of fans, my face would probably have been far redder a few moments later, as I heard the bad news.

'Sorry,' said my bright hope, looking very pleased. 'Cliff is too busy to talk to anyone. He's visiting a hospital next, and a school, and heaven knows what else.' But heaven must have known about me, too, as I did my best to merge fast into the crush again, feeling lots of serve-you-right smiles aimed my way. Because suddenly I felt a strong nudge to ask at the other end of that very long table, despite Cliff looking a lost cause by now. It was all to do with whether I could trust God to guide me minute by minute, or not. As he seemed to have set the whole interview situation up, letting me know about Cliff in the nick of time, I should be expecting him to see it through. And I was beginning to discover that if I didn't let disobedience or disbelief get in his way in my life then he always completed what he'd begun. All I needed was to keep hearing his still, small voice.

So I glanced again at the top end of the table. The

face of the lean and lofty gentleman seemed to look grimmer than ever. I thought that maybe standing there all this time was getting to his corns. But at least he wasn't getting them trodden on like some of us. And even if he were to say 'no' like his friend, my asking would have made a little diversion for him, and more entertainment for the masses.

So I pushed boldly over in his direction and waited until his colleague wasn't looking my way.

'Is there any chance of interviewing Cliff for local radio?' I smiled, managing to sound confident, in spite of knowing full well what this forbidding man's answer would be. At first I thought his answering smile was sarcastic. But no! 'I guess Cliff might like a rest by now,' he said. 'Just wait while I ask him.' And while I waited I thought of how deceptive appearances can be. Some of us just happen to be born with miserable faces, disguising sunny dispositions. This man can *afford* to be sunny, too, I realised, as my new friend questioned Cliff, because suddenly it hit me that while his colleague at the other end was probably the shop manager—not knowing Cliff at all—this one must be Cliff's manager from the way he was cheerfully cuffing him. 'It's not what you know but who you know' came over loud and clear as he beckoned me to Cliff's side. The shop manager gave me a 'Cheek!' sort of look as I walked across, but a look tinged with admiration too. Admiration that should have gone to my Manager really—but I was giving him plenty of that!

So, in no time at all, I was pretending to be a hard-baked atheist, just like my friend Kate, with all sorts of suspicions about Cliff. And it must have been a convincing act as I harangued him about his money and

his single lifestyle and his professed faith. He answered
Kate and all the other doubters really brilliantly, with all
his customary wit, and finished by urging me to examine
my life and get right with God myself! Then he settled
down again to sign for his eager fans. But as I hastily
packed up the recording machine at the side of him,
with one eye on the clock, I suddenly thought how Cliff
might just be wasting a prayer on my obviously lost state.

So, to let him know I was only the devil's advocate I
whispered a surprise 'Praise the Lord!' in his ear. And
maybe because meeting another Jesus-person unexpectedly without sharing the fact that you're brother and
sister is really sad, Cliff spun round with a smile that said
it all; and as he did I celebrated a surprise victory.
Because once I'd have found that biblical instruction
about being no respecter of persons (James 2:1–10)
really difficult to carry out. But as the crowds around
wondered what I'd whispered, I realised that I was no
more thrilled with Cliff's reaction than with the delight
of discovering that the bus driver, half an hour earlier,
was a born-again Christian too. Those little lapel fishes
can be really useful fellowship spreaders!

Anyway, with Cliff still signing, and me soon singing
as I sped off to the surgery (the Lord arranging that the
timetable left me just the necessary minute or two to
reach it), the first words to greet me as I panted over the
threshold, level with the first patient, were: 'Oh, Mrs
Cook, how wonderful!' It was Rachel, the dental nurse,
looking delirious with joy. 'I saw you there with Cliff,'
she beamed. 'I'd been waiting all lunch-time for him to
sign my book. Can we just hear how the interview went
while you scrub-up?' So the patient came in to listen,
too. 'I'm sure you'll love it,' Rachel smiled at the

bemused elderly gentleman as I started to examine his dentures to a background of Cliff's beliefs.

And that's how all our patients looked through the afternoon—bemused! They kept arriving in the waiting room to be greeted by a tape recorder rendering Rachel's umpteenth playback of everybody's favourite star—she hoped! Without knowing Jesus herself she was making a brilliant job of proclaiming him relevant to the people who came in. And as Cliff's inspired skill both with words and ideas communicated to each new patient that Jesus really is alive (and to me through our thin surgery walls), I was able to add silent prayer power to the impetus of the message. And then I prayed inwardly again as the patients sat in the dental chair, for blessing for them—blessings in every way. And especially for their teeth, of course—the faith-filled dentist being in a perfect position for laying-on of hands when the occasion demands.

Maybe it was something to do with the waiting room warm-up that afternoon, but one middle-aged lady patient shared with me her worry about a serious health complaint; so, for just half a minute, with punctuality for the next patient in mind, I was able to tell her about the healing power of Jesus for any ailment at all, great or small. And somehow I felt led to pray aloud with her that her chronically diseased tooth-root attachments would be healed too. She left the surgery with the prescription to praise God for his healing power, and to get to church too, along with the more usual sort of dental prescription clutched in her hands.

It was wonderful to discover on her return to the surgery, a week or two later, that her loose teeth were indeed growing miraculously tighter, with her much improved oral hygiene backing the prayer-and-praise power. (I'd explained that the ligaments of loosened teeth cannot naturally tighten themselves, but that good oral hygiene prevents them becoming worse. And that little ailments like loose teeth are meant to be prayed about just as much as cancer and other serious diseases, because God has more than enough power to cope with every imperfection on the face of this planet—when asked.)

I left the practice for another shortly after that memorable encounter so I never did make sure about the other half of that lady's healing, long term. But I did ascertain she'd discovered the most important healing of all when, on her last visit to me, she told me how on her first she'd forced herself to the surgery in fear and trembling, having always been terrified of dentistry. At the waiting room door her courage failed her and she was about to turn away again when she heard Cliff's voice inside, loud and clear. She was an ardent fan and just had to push open the door to discover what was happening, and she was ardent enough to stay put when she realised that what she'd somehow missed at the bookshop, she could make up for in our waiting room—over and over!

She had sailed into the surgery on a wave of euphoria to see the lucky dentist who'd been interviewing her heart throb. And when, weeks later, we'd finally finished sorting out her teeth, she realised she'd even more than losing her fear of dentistry and rediscovering physical health to thank Cliff for! Maybe for Cliff it was just another interview among the thousands that don't often produce personal comeback, but for Kate, and for Rachel, and for our newly faith-filled friend, it was 'just what the dentist ordered'—and more besides.

9

Seeing Is Believing

It was a great day for Jenny—the day she took off on her European tour. She'd been living with us for about a year and had become so much part of the family that she was like a daughter to me. So much so that I had to remind myself that, at almost twenty, she didn't need tucking up at night like the younger ones! In fact she was often doing the tucking up herself as our unofficial nanny for new little Stephanie. Jenny was such a gregarious and caring person—having grown up as a daughter of the manse in a very loving family—that she'd needed three farewell parties before she left us to become part of a Christian drama group, travelling all over Europe. But now it was time to give Jenny one last hug, as her 'farewell lunch' friends gathered for a photo in our front room.

David and I were excused because we already featured often enough in her photo album, and anyway David had to be driven back to his community dentistry office as his car was in dock. So a threesome hug with our 'adopted daughter' said it all, and en route to the town centre David and I reminisced together about how

much love the Lord had channelled to us through Jenny
while we'd known her. And maybe it was our joy in
Jenny, and in the Lord's love, that led to my response
over a strange surprise encounter a minute or two after
dropping David at work.

I was driving round a very busy roundabout in the city
centre, in a hurry to get back home because I was due at
the surgery in half an hour, and a friend was going to
drop *me* at work too. (She needed to borrow my car to
transport an elderly friend to hospital so I was going to
catch the bus back home after work, while teenage
Matthew held the fort, as the children returned from
school.) Anyway, as I circled the roundabout I saw the
fattest, dirtiest, scruffiest tramp I'd ever seen! And
giving him a second glance, I was amazed to experience
a wave of compassion flowing over me for him. It was as
if I was seeing him as the happy, fulfilled person he
could have become if life had treated him—and he had
treated life—differently. And knowing it still wasn't too
late for his lifestyle to be transformed by my living and
loving Lord really did move me. But not far enough. So
I made my excuses.

'Honestly, Lord,' I prayed, 'if I could only stop the car
and tell that man about you I would, like a shot, but I'm
here on the roundabout. I can't stop and I'm nearly late
for work!' So I prayed for my tramp instead, hoping it
didn't seem too much like second best to the Lord.
Arriving home, I left Matt a note about looking after the
older children after school, knowing little Stephanie was
safe with Grandma. And I mentally noted that I must
endeavour to catch the 5 pm bus back (my last patient
being booked for 4.30 that afternoon), especially as
John was at the infuriating stage of baiting his elders

and betters. And I'd not had time to prepare much dinner, either.

All went well that afternoon until the last patient arrived. The poor man had a really difficult molar to remove and my skill and muscle power were seemingly getting me nowhere at all. On top of it all, that bus was looking more and more impossible to catch. So I silently prayed the most powerful prayer I could think of. It was, 'Help! Help me, Lord!' And despite my failing faith, he did! With the tooth safely extracted and the patient happy again, I flew out of the surgery knowing I had five minutes before the bus departed. But, as I threaded my way between the pedestrians and the heavy rush-hour traffic towards the crowded bus-stop, my hopes were dashed. It was only two minutes to 5 pm but there was the bus, early for once, rounding the corner to the stop, and I still had the dual carriageway to cross, and the lights were at red. Calling 'Help' this time made no difference—the bus sailed away just as I finally made it to the other side.

I was so incredulous that the Lord had allowed the bus to go when he'd helped me with the almost impossible molar, that I still walked towards the bus-shelter, even though I knew there wouldn't be another bus for half an hour. It was a beautiful summer's day and I should have started walking in the opposite direction, with all that time before the next bus, to reduce the bus fare. But somehow I felt I must have seen a mirage— that the Lord couldn't possibly be so inconsistent as to let the bus go early when he was in the middle of helping me to arrive home on time. Surely the real bus would materialise at any moment.

It didn't, of course, but a second later I saw why.

Around the corner of the bus-shelter ambled the fattest, dirtiest, scruffiest—not to mention smelliest—tramp I'd seen earlier that day. 'Lord,' I breathed, 'so that's why you had me miss that bus. You need me to mean what I said about talking to that tramp. Well, Lord, at least you're bound to be looking after our household if you've gone to all this trouble to arrange such an amazingly timed meeting. I just can't believe it! He was five miles away when I saw him this lunch-time. How do you do it? But you'll have to give me the right words for him— whatever they are.'

The divinely directed gentleman of the road was walking along my bus route. Though I hesitated for half a second, I was aware that I was honour-bound to walk with him, even if I did see someone I knew! And to talk with him, and tell him what I would have told him at the roundabout. With half an hour to do it I began with a few pleasantries.

His name was Alan. And though he looked a bit surprised to be walking along with such a posh-sounding lady (I was educated at a private school till I was seven, and the accent stuck) he was soon chatting like an old friend. And I was delighted to discover that Alan's rough, tough life hadn't dented his cheerfulness—nor his alert mind.

He entertained me for a while with his adventures, between sleeping under the stars and feasting in soup kitchens. It all sounded too good to be true—and it probably was! He'd been at it so long I wondered if he'd been one of the vagrants whose feet I'd washed as a student in Leeds, at the celebrated St George's crypt. After a while, with the hot midsummer sun on our backs reminding me of God's absolute love for us both we got

round to talking about Jesus. 'I wuz allus sent ter
Sunday School as a lad,' he said, 'but I jus' grew art of all
that lark.' So I told him how it was really far more of a
lark than he ever realised. And that whether we're
tramps, or dentists who've missed the bus, walking with
Jesus makes life so exciting that any other way is
self-destructive boredom by comparison. That led to a
lively discussion in which I could share the agonies and
the ecstasies of letting Jesus run our lives.

By the time we'd been walking for half an hour,
asking Alan whether he'd like to pray with me to the
Person who made him just came naturally. Soon he was
asking Jesus to come into his rough-and-ready heart,
and to make him the new creation I'd told him about.
Still a tramp, of course, but a tramp for the Lord! And
then he went out of my life, the bus arriving on cue.
Though I've looked for him a lot I've never managed to
find him. But although following up Alan hasn't been
possible, I know that God's divine appointment system
will have continued to operate in his life. So he'll keep
on bumping into the people who can help him grow up
in Jesus. I'm definitely looking forward to meeting him
when these bodies of ours have finally finished with
walking for good. (Which makes me wonder whether
our heavenly bodies will ever need baths. I hope not, for
Alan's sake—and ours!)

Seeing him walking towards that bus-stop was one of
the most astonishing moments of my life. And it encouraged me, if I needed any encouragement, to know that I
could trust God when work occasionally keeps me away
from home longer than I'd like—though only if I know
he's behind the delay, not me.

One of the reasons why I sometimes arrive home

from work a little later than usual is because I pick up fruit and vegetables for our family's healthy eating regime—as well as their healthy appetites! Halfway home from work I often call at a greengrocer's where there's a very good reminder of how our employment can be part of God's outreach. Behind the counter stands Jackie, who ministers loving care and concern to anyone in need, along with the very best fruit and vegetables. Time and again I've seen her being the Lord's salt and light to the customers. And particularly, one Saturday, for me.

I'd been suffering for two days from a migraine, and the daggers-in-my-head feeling seemed to be even more unbearable after bending over patients all morning. I knew it must be my fault, for indulging in too much of either cheese, chocolate, bacon or caffeine—the triggers that set it off—but it was comforting that as I walked into the greengrocer's Jackie said sympathetically, 'Are you all right, Hilary? You don't look very well.' And she kept giving me concerned looks as I waited in the queue. Soon she was serving me in a way I hadn't expected; a really biblical way.

Walking round to my side of the counter in the now almost empty shop, but obviously unconcerned about anyone else coming in, she laid her hands on my head. Then she asked God to release me from the headache, and commanded the migraine to go, in Jesus' name. Immediately the nausea disappeared, and by the time I reached home ten minutes later all the pain had gone too, and the migraine was only a memory. The memory I'll happily keep, however, is of Jackie listening hard to the Lord in the middle of her work—and then obeying his nudge to pray, whatever people thought.

Actually, it probably costs Jackie more in terms of courage to come to the surgery than it did to walk round the counter that day, dentists in general being her least favourite people, as I could tell the first time I walked into her shop and she discovered all about me through seeing my fish badge. The most nervous patient I've ever had came to me through a work contact too—when a teacher friend told her junior school colleague, Liz, that I could anaesthetise nerves of both sorts very well! Liz turned out to be a wonderful prayer warrior. And when she no longer needed to worry about her teeth and their treatment, she was even more free to concentrate on moving mountains prayer-wise. So now we have a two-way Wednesday lunch-time prayer get-together, for Liz's classroom and my surgery to be more and more God's territory for transforming lives in every way.

Another 'worker' on my route home from the surgery is Ruth, a middle-aged member of our church, whose front room contains a feast for hungry and thirsty brothers and sisters. Not that she serves non-stop refreshments, but she and her husband have built up an enormous lending library of Christian books, as well as tapes and videos. A year or so ago Ruth's husband received his promotion to glory, but Ruth has continued their work of sharing the good news and refreshing weary Christians, sending tapes and literature all over the world. And though she's weary herself sometimes, without John to help her, it's work that's far too valuable, for Christians and non-Christians, to think of stopping. Like many other indispensable workers, Ruth doesn't get paid by the world for the work she does. But God's remuneration, though often unpredictable in its timing, is always breathtaking in its accuracy for covering any need just when it needs to. And knowing God as she does, Ruth is often nudged to pray with someone who thought they'd only come for a book or video—and to look forward to hearing about God's answer when the item is returned!

Occasionally, in my work, I find I'm directed by an inner urge, straight from the Holy Spirit, to offer to pray for a patient. I always test such promptings before I say anything by asking the Lord to have someone interrupt me if I'm wrong. And most of all by checking the peace which is meant to be the umpire in our hearts (Colossians 3:15). That way I see whether the suggestion is just my good idea, mischief sown in my mind by the enemy of our souls, or an instruction from my heavenly Father via the Holy Spirit who's taken up residence in me. It's strange that any dental surgery prayers I pray usually seem to be for other parts of the anatomy than teeth—as if the Lord doesn't mean to deprive me of the satisfaction of doing my bit!

But it's gratifying to think that our dental chair has been the scene of healing from spondylosis in the neck, acute depression and, more than once, migraine! In fact, the dental nurses have learned such a lot about what Jesus can do I guess one of them can pray for me if I get migraine again now!

The other work I'm involved in, apart from homemaking, keeps me safely in the heart of the home. I'm referring to my writing. And its solitary nature means there aren't too many 'seeing is believing' miracles involved. God-incidences, as distinct from coincidences, usually happen where people are relating to each other in a way that he can use—whether we're going the extra mile, just having fun together, or

speaking the truth in love—and sometimes out of it!
And because relationships are God's greatest invention,
especially the human/divine variety, there's no thrill
quite as great as hearing God's voice, audibly or
otherwise. Well, that still, small voice occasionally guides
my writing, but I've never become a skilled enough
typist for typing to be anything but a slog. So I was
delighted one day to hear how God had rewarded my
one-time secretary friend Janet for all her typewritten
labours of love on behalf of an author friend of hers.

I first met Janet over the phone, when she rang to see
whether I'd be on a women's committee she was chairing
here in Sheffield for the Billy Graham mission. She
seemed both down-to-earth and inspired—an exciting
person to work with. Recently arrived from Bedford, I
discovered Janet had been typing out books for the
writer Marion Stroud for some years. Marion is the wife
of a dental surgeon whom we had met professionally
years before, and it seemed appropriate to me that two
such gifted women should work together. I was soon
being inspired myself by Janet's imaginative ideas, and
by her meticulous attention to detail. But it was God's
attention to detail that really took my breath away in
Janet's 'seeing is believing' story.

It all started when Janet decided she'd call in at
Sheffield's Christian Literature Crusade bookshop to
see if the last book she'd typed for Marion was on the
shelves yet. It was one of a glossy coffee table type
collection, the title *The Gift of Years*, proclaiming in
words and pictures the joys of growing old gracefully.
Christmas was a few weeks away and the book would be
an ideal present for her parents, living down south. She
soon spotted it and hurried home before the children

arrived from school, putting the CLC parcel on the hall table. 'Mum, can we open this for you?' Jeremy and Rachel called to her a few minutes later as they hung up their coats. 'OK, but keep it clean. It's a Christmas present,' she replied. A second later they shouted, 'Mum, come and look! There's Grandma and Grandpa on the cover of this book.' 'They can't be,' laughed Janet, meeting the children at the kitchen door. 'But you're right. They are!'

There in the middle of a beautiful woodland clearing, glowing golden-brown with all the colours of autumn, were two tiny figures with their backs to the camera. The woman was sitting on a bench with the man standing behind her, arm upraised in praise of all the beauty around him. Immediately, Janet knew it had to be her mum and dad. She didn't know where the photo had been taken, but she knew who must have arranged it—her friend Marion. *What a lovely surprise*, she thought, *for all the typing I've enjoyed being able to do for her*.

But Marion knew nothing about it when Janet phoned that night. 'Maybe the publishers might be able to throw some light on the matter,' she suggested. 'But usually they just choose an appropriate picture from their photographic stock.'

So, all of a sudden, Janet knew exactly how it had happened, and it took her breath away. The coincidence involved was too great for anyone but her heavenly Father to have arranged, which made the 'thank you surprise' even more amazingly special. And she knew that it would be an equally wonderful surprise for her parents to receive the ultimate in personalised Christmas presents too! Especially as it turned out that they had no idea their photo had been taken that glorious day. And now they could share the day with so many others, at home and abroad—along with their neighbours, who never knew that God even noticed book covers!

When we see our work, as well as our play, God's way it makes believing for it to be blessed and used by him very easy. And seeing really is believing when God is at work. One of my favourite verses is: 'God works for those who wait for him' (Isaiah 64:4, TLB). And over and over in my varied work I find that waiting patiently for his purposes to unfold produces amazing dividends in the way of healed bodies, souls and spirits.

Just so long as I don't spoil everything by trying to hurry ahead of him, that is. And whether I'm washing the pots, or interviewing an Archbishop, I need to remember to do it to please my main Employer—and no one else. When I meet difficulties at work, from drudgery or self-doubt to disagreement with a fellow-worker (Christian or not), I need especially to remember to praise my way out of the fog into the sunshine of God's solutions. That way I see all my toil working out to mean more and more neighbours coming to know him. Sometimes it happens very slowly, but God works to a timetable that we can't work out, but we can work with. And it's really brilliant that if we stay with it, like Janet, we won't be believing our eyes either!

WORK-OUT 3
Neighbours at Work

Live I, so live I . . . to my neighbour honestly.
(Henry Wadsworth Longfellow, 1907–82)

We need not bid, for cloistered cell
Our neighbour and our work farewell
Nor strive to wind ourselves too high
For sinful man beneath the sky.
(John Keble, 1792–1866)

1. WORKING FLAT OUT
We see the nation's work needs fluctuate from a flooded employment market to a need to recruit retired people, as the number of young people of employable age rises and falls.

Read 1 Corinthians 3:5–15.

(a) How can we find God's specific work for us?
(b) Should a Christian always expect job satisfaction—for instance, being a housewife with little children at home? (How can a housewife become a homemaker?)
(c) Is it right to witness for the Lord in our employer's time?
(d) Would we be willing to risk offering to pray for a colleague with migraine at work there and then?

2. CLIFF-HANGING CELEBRATION
Read Colossians 3:22–4:6.

(a) How strict should Christians be over ethical standards at work—for instance, 'borrowing' a Biro from the firm—especially after working unpaid overtime?

124

(b) Is it right for Christians to want to find themselves Christian doctors, plumbers, etc. and to seek employment only in Christian firms?

(c) How much are you influenced by people's appearance, at work or anywhere else?

(d) How many people where you work (or otherwise relate to people) know you are a Christian?

3. SEEING IS BELIEVING

The number of people living on the streets in this country is estimated to be around the 8,000 mark, a large proportion being young people, sleeping often under cardboard, eating from bins, and exposed to many temptations. Often with no homes to return to, the lack of a fixed address means no government help.

Read Isaiah 58:6–12 and James 1:22–27.

(a) What can the church do about the homelessness problem?

(b) What is the difference between coincidences and God-incidences?

(c) How often do you pray, and praise God, during your work? And could you begin a prayer and fellowship group at your workplace (if there isn't one already), asking God to lead you to someone else willing to start it with you?

(d) How can verse 6 of Isaiah 58 apply today? Should being a Christian inevitably have political overtones?

Praise Point: 'Present yourself to God as one approved, a workman who does not need to be ashamed' (2 Timothy 2:15, NIV).

PART FOUR
Neighbours in the Church

10

Churchgoers Can't Be Choosy

'Methodist is best' was increasingly my watchword through my developing years, ever since our local chapel became my spiritual home at the age of three. As I advanced through the Sunday School I became more and more sure that even the heavenly hosts would be bound to use the Methodist hymn-book. And anyway, whoever would want to belong to any other brand of church when they could choose to inherit the spiritual legacy of Britain's greatest evangelist and its most prolific hymn-writer, joining brotherly forces to convert and renew a desperately decadent nation?

But it wasn't until my heart was 'strangely warmed'—like John Wesley's—in my mid-teens through a schools' evangelistic holiday in the Lake District that I really discovered what John and Charles were on about. Then at last I could understand John's brilliance in building and leading the Methodism he'd never intended, and Charles' anointing for heavenly hymn-writing. An anointing shared by other contributors to the Methodist hymn-book too. That anointing provided my first spiritual experience actually, a few years before I finally saw the light.

It was when I was promoted to the senior Sunday School class at eleven, and the teacher turned us to number 334 in the hymn-book, an old gospel hymn written by Elizabeth Clephane with music by Ira Sankey. 'There were ninety and nine that safely lay in the shelter of the fold . . .' we began to sing, unenthusiastically as usual. Then, halfway through the first verse, tears started to spill down my cheeks. The thought of Jesus caring enough to risk everything for one lost lamb, when he had ninety-nine already, was just too much for me. But for the next thirty years I couldn't understand why that particular hymn should have revealed a little glimpse of the strength of God's love, when for all the rest of my time in Sunday School I was basically clueless and oblivious to it.

Then recently someone lent me a magazine that gave me the answer. It seems that Sankey, the Victorian revivalist singer, was travelling up to Edinburgh by train one day to join Dwight Moody, his fellow-American evangelist partner, in a mission there. On the journey he noticed a printed card on the compartment floor and, picking it up, discovered the words of the hymn that made me cry. It was a poem at the time, newly printed, but a tune quickly presented itself to Sankey as a possibility for the inspiring words. So, alone in the carriage, he sang it over to himself. Then he put the card in his pocket and forgot about it.

It was some hours later that it suddenly came to mind again. Sankey was sitting on the Edinburgh stage while his friend Moody addressed the vast crowd, before turning to Sankey for that night's solo. Suddenly Sankey knew the Lord was telling him to forget the song he'd prepared and to fish Miss Clephane's poem out of his pocket and sing that instead! He was certain he'd never remember the tune consistently, and was in a cold sweat as the seconds ticked by to his solo spot. But he knew the source of that strong inner voice, and that he had no choice if he wanted God to bless his ministry that night—even if he did dry up in the middle of the first verse. So Sankey stood and opened his mouth, and found that the remembered first few notes were followed by a really inspiring melody. A melody that he proceeded to reproduce perfectly for all five verses.

So now I know why that specially anointed hymn started to turn me towards the Saviour I wasn't going to meet for five more years. And I guess Sankey's willingness to appear a fool for Christ must have started to rub off on me too, as I sang those words and started to weep.

All my Methodist experience, though, left me totally unprepared to discover that other denominations might share different gifts and different strengths, to add to our joint riches in Christ. And it wasn't until our neighbourhood house group came into being that I discovered that Catholic, Anglican, Baptist, Pentecostal, United Reformed, house church and any other sort of church member could all add to our corporate worship in different ways. And that I could enjoy far more fellowship with a born-again Catholic, for instance, than with a Methodist who hadn't yet progressed from just knowing about Jesus to knowing him personally for themselves.

As a student in the Christian Union I'd had practice at worshipping with quite a few different denominations already. And when we were newly married, David and I had taught each week in a United Reformed church, helping to lead the largest Sunday School in Derbyshire (with a scarcity of believing adults we didn't have much option). But even so, I still didn't feel ready for the great leap forward the Lord was preparing David and myself for. We were becoming more and more sure, when we moved house into the city, that we should attend the nearest local church so that we could support it on the spot. I just wished, though, that St Oswald's didn't have to be so high Anglican—totally the wrong side of the non-conformist divide for me. And our first few months there seemed impossible.

Gradually, however, the Lord taught us how to worship him as freely in liturgy with genuflecting and crucifixes involved as in a more informal Methodist 'hymn-sandwich' service. And we really learned to appreciate our 'high Anglican is best' new-found friends. Because of God's call to us there in St Oswald's, David and I were soon running a Youth Club, and getting involved with a family centre as that materialised too. And with David as the church treasurer and me a co-opted Sunday School teacher, we both learned that availability to go God's way can set us free from needing to choose where we worship—into the glorious liberty of being denomination-less at heart, and happy with it.

And, of course, we soon learned that the Lord's love being shared among us is the most important need in any church—high, low, or whatever else. St Oswald's supplies plenty of that precious commodity—and in practical as well as spiritual ways, as this letter showed when it appeared in the parish magazine from David and myself.

Dear Friends,
    This is a thank-you letter to very many people in our wonderfully warm parish (even though it is January!).

Our hearts have been greatly encouraged by all the practical care and prayer that went out to our six-year-old son John, and us, as he underwent open-heart surgery six weeks ago. So we'd like to share with you some of the wonderful answers God provided as we all prayed together.

One of the first answers to prayer was that John survived what turned out to be a very difficult operation—building a new artery between the heart and the lungs, as the old one wasn't functioning at all. (The substance used was Gortex—the stretchable plastic that also makes wonderful winter boots!) The surgeon also found that the shunt-artery created for John when he was six weeks old, to increase oxygenation, was now non-functional too. So he should have been totally starved of oxygen—except for an astonishingly high number of tiny, threadlike channels which had gradually opened up between the heart exit and the lungs. We saw that as a miracle—God's response to John receiving laying-on of hands for healing, in St Oswald's and elsewhere.

But God had more miracles in store for us there at Killingbeck Hospital, near Leeds, where I stayed with John for a fortnight (while David and our talented teenage friend, Jenny, kept the rest of our family very happy with life). And not just the miracle of using the surgeons' skills in an amazing way, but miracles of hearts made new in everlasting ways too.

It all started in intensive care. My faith had already been raised in the parents' waiting room. That's where I met Evelyn—as the night-shift changed hands and we waited for the nurses to tell us we could return to our boys' bedsides. But suddenly Evelyn's son's nurse put his head round the door and said Paul was in trouble, so could we stay put for a while. Evelyn, of course, was terribly worried. And when I suggested prayer—having already talked to Evelyn about the Lord after she'd asked how I could stay so calm—it seemed to her the natural thing to do. So it was wonderfully timed for us, just a minute after we'd said 'Amen', that the nurse appeared again saying, 'Everything looks to be fine now, so do come through.'

Arriving back at John's bedside I discovered that the little girl, just two years old, in the bed next to John was in a desperate condition. Pat's heart operation had been successfully performed a fort-night before, but she still hadn't begun to breathe again, except through a ventilator. Every time the staff tried to encourage her to breathe normally by switching off the ventilator, the response was nil. John had a ventilator tube down his throat, too, but I could see that he was 'in the pink', literally, after being blue from birth, and I knew that it was Pat who was needing my prayers just then, not John.

Suddenly I had an idea. 'I'm just going to the phone,' I told John's nurse, 'to ask some Christian friends back home in Sheffield to pray for Patricia.' I thought I'd better explain why I was leaving John's side so heartlessly, only half an hour after his ope-ration. He'd be oblivious to the world for twenty-four hours so I knew he wouldn't miss me. After relaying the message I sat down again by John, and continued to pray for poor little Patricia.

'I am worried about Pat,' said her nurse to John's nurse, half an hour later. 'She's always so sunny and good, but she's been in distress for the last half hour and I just can't see what's wrong.' *Oh dear*, I thought, *my prayer is making things worse!* The surgeon couldn't see what was wrong either when she called him a minute later. 'I'll have to switch off the ventilator for a second,' he said, 'and see if that gives us any clue.' So he did. And—lo and behold—Pat began to breathe! From then on the ventilator was redundant. 'I'm sure she must have been trying to breathe ever since your friends started to pray,' exclaimed John's nurse, 'but the ventilator wouldn't let her. Well, I was an agnostic till just now—but not any more!' And she proceeded to tell all the intensive care staff how she'd seen a miracle. The story spread back to Pat and John's ward. And soon all sorts of people—parents and staff—who had almost never given God a thought before, began to ask questions. And sometimes to pray themselves. So we continued to see our loving heavenly Father's plans unfold in amazing ways in answer to your prayers.

Heartfelt thanks to you all.

David, Hilary and family.

One of those amazing ways made me so glad we belonged to St Oswald's. John had sailed through the operation and through intensive care with no trouble at all. But five days after the operation he became really ill with high temperatures, no appetite at all, and no interest in living. 'That's exactly what happened to our James,' said the concerned young mum of the little boy in the next bed. 'And he's been here for three whole months now, and the doctors just can't clear up the infection on his heart valves.'

I'd been passing on James' name for concerted prayer

back home but he was still looking as white and ill as ever. I looked at John and wondered however else I could pray for God to heal him—and James too. I was even working at fasting, along with prayer, and plenty of praise thrown in too. But all of a sudden that afternoon God showed me I didn't need formulas any more, only the sort of trust that kept praising him anyway, through everything. And he showed me through Roy, our vicar at St Oswald's.

I was taking a well wrapped-up John in his wheelchair along the hospital corridor, to see if the toys at the monthly sale-of-work might give him an interest in living again. And suddenly round a corner strode the reassuring shape of Roy, having travelled thirty miles to see how John was doing. The amazing fact was that from the moment John saw Roy, or maybe, more importantly, Roy saw John, it was as if God had sent him as the human channel of his superhuman power.

At that time John hardly knew our new vicar but he immediately sat up, lost his temperature, began to smile and, as soon as we arrived back at the bedside, began to eat too! He never looked back, and I was only sorry that newly-arrived Roy couldn't possibly realise quite what a mighty miracle God had used him for! Especially miraculous—and heart-rending—as we continued to see James deteriorate after exactly the same symptoms as John but beginning all those months ago. But we, and St Oswald's, and many others, continued to pray for James, and some time later, when all hope seemed gone, God used a last chance, life-or-death operation to restore James to the very lively boy he is today.

So gradually I realised that the church I wouldn't have chosen was able to be as much a channel of God's power as any other place where people are wanting to put him first in their lives. And I realised, too, that God probably didn't notice denominations at all—only which particular people in them had become his personal property! St Oswald's might have been far more formal than the fellowship meetings I was increasingly enjoying, but the God of surprises was able to bring about the same breathtaking miracles among the believers, even though worship was expressed so differently. And the experience of Mavis was a case in point.

She was training to be a pastoral worker for the parish, and working really hard running the family centre, as well as in worship commitments. One Friday afternoon she was hurrying up the church drive when she slipped and heard a loud snap in the back of her left leg. Suddenly she could hardly walk, and was suffering enough pain to cause a trip to the hospital where a torn tendon was diagnosed. The doctor said, 'You won't be able to walk on this leg for three weeks,' and bandaged it tightly from top to bottom. 'What a weekend for it to happen!' smiled Mavis ruefully when she saw the vicar later that day. And Roy agreed.

There was a church excursion the next day by coach to Holy Island, off the Northumberland coast. It was especially appropriate as Holy Island was one of St Oswald's ancient headquarters for his northern kingdom. (He was a sixth-century king, as well as a saint.) And then on Sunday Mavis was due to be initiated into her pastoral training back home at a special service in St Oswald's, taken by the Archdeacon of Sheffield.

'Oh well, at least we've the church wheelchair,' laughed Roy, in his usual infectious way. But this time he wasn't joking. The wheelchair that some kind benefactor had placed at the back of the large church for emergencies was both unwieldy and inflexible. But it worked. And the next day Roy kindly pushed his parish worker-to-be all over Holy Island, and finally to the ancient church there, for a celebratory communion service.

Mavis remembered that St Oswald was renowned for God's gift of healing flowing through him to many in need all those centuries ago. And it crossed her mind that people had been healed through taking communion before, and through Roy's ministry too. She didn't allow herself to be too disappointed though when she needed pushing back to the coach after the service. But there were still those on the coach with plenty of faith to see Mavis' leg healed—particularly Brian, a doctor, and his wife Joan, who'd been praying for a miracle.

The journey turned into an extra time of joyful worship as the miles sped by, and somebody started off the chorus 'Peter and John went to pray', about the healing of the lame man at the Temple Gate, as an encouragement for Mavis. She had a seat to herself to give her rigid left leg a bit more space, but suddenly Brian went to sit next to her, and they chatted together about the joys of Holy Island.

Then Mavis grew tired, as Brian returned to his seat, and nodded off for a minute or two to be awakened by a wonderful warmth flooding her leg, and a great feeling of lightness where the pain had been. She had an overwhelming urge to 'rise up and walk' as the song said. And to her joy, the Lord had so timed her healing that at that very moment the coach driver was turning into a service station for refreshments all round. Seeing Mavis start to her feet had friends hurrying forward to help, but they fell back in amazement as Mavis demonstrated her healing to everyone, most of whom had never seen a miracle before. And the coach driver was lost for words as he replaced the redundant wheelchair in the boot.

The archdeacon had happened to be on the excursion too, on another coach, and had commiserated over Mavis needing to attend her authorisation service the next day in a wheelchair. So he was probably more incredulous than anyone the next morning as he saw Mavis hurrying down the aisle towards him, just as if he'd dreamed the happenings of the day before. 'Isn't it good, though,' said Mavis, 'that it all happened on such a very public weekend? The whole church family, and more besides, can't fail to know now that Jesus really is alive. And that he heals today just like two thousand years ago.' St Oswald would certainly be pleased!

11

Open House—Open Hearts

It's no wonder that loving your neighbour as yourself can be hardest of all in church fellowships. The enemy of our souls has a vested interest in rendering churches as divided as possible. He'll often use jealousy and resentment to do it. And people being too touchy. That way God's potentially powerful freedom fighters in our neighbourhoods become captive themselves—to back-biting, insularity and bitterness. Divisions don't *need* to include animosity, however. Churches can divide over simple differences of doctrine, or opinion, and members can still remain in a carefully guarded attitude of love for each other. If two local congregations are then produced where there was only one, as peacefully as possible and with continuing care for each other, then Satan's strategy has totally failed—and God's kingdom can grow in even more glorious ways. But the former sort of split is all too common, and we need to practise preserving our oneness in Jesus, often at the price of letting go of long-held traditions and ambitions. Especially, for instance, when we've always played the organ or arranged the flowers, and someone more talented turns up. It can hurt to hand over; particularly if the person is less talented than we are but needs to be encouraged in usefulness to the fellowship. Sometimes we need a practical test to work out our motivation in service— whether we're working to impress other people, or to please God. As a very honest church neighbour shared with me the other day.

'I arrived really early at the prayer meeting and found I was first there. The caretaker hadn't put the chairs in the customary circle, and I suddenly realised that I could do it instead. But as I was halfway through I started to slow down, because it occurred to me that I might finish my little task too soon—before anyone else arrived! And I didn't want people to think the caretaker had done the job, when it was my hard work instead. Just in time I realised what childish pride I was slipping into, and hurried myself up. And then the Lord was able to feed into my mind that I could pray for whoever was going to occupy each chair as I completed the circle. So I was set free from myself into really loving my neighbour.'

Even when we haven't put the chairs out, it's still a good plan at any church meeting to begin by silently offering a prayer for each person there. A prayer for each one to be blessed and a blessing, one by one. You can tell from that comment that we belong to a smallish church fellowship, but even in larger bodies, praying for individuals around us at the very beginning of the service or meeting is a great habit to get into. And it's also a great antidote to negative feelings over noisy children, lazy church members, or irritatingly enthusiastic brothers and sisters. That reminds me of young Stephanie spending her Saturday money on gobstoppers. But Stephanie had aptly misheard. 'I'm getting

God-stoppers,' she explained. 'Then God can stop me and John getting into trouble for talking in the service tomorrow.'

Talking in itself, though, unguarded by God, can lead to tremendous trouble for relationships in the church. If we know the motivation for our words isn't love, we'd better keep silent. And when we, or other people, have caused trouble, unwittingly or not, then 'least said, soonest mended' is a good watchword, after all necessary forgiveness has been asked—especially when we feel wronged rather than in the wrong. Asking forgiveness for any unintentional distress caused, and refusing to vindicate ourselves, can lead to more availability to God for his 'grain of wheat' (John 12:24) power to flow through us to a desperately needy world. And it's worth that dying to ourselves when we read about the end results:

> The Spirit of the Lord is on me, because He has anointed me, to preach good news to the poor. He has sent me to proclaim freedom for the prisoners, and recovery of sight for the blind, to release the oppressed, to proclaim the year of the Lord's favour.

They are doubly important words for the church, coming twice in God's word. Jesus repeated them in his first sermon in his home town of Nazareth, from Isaiah 61, as we read in Luke 4:18–19. And though they particularly apply to Jesus, they mirror his instructions to us, his hands and feet—able to be used in miracle-working power for this sad planet. Individual churches are increasingly seeing that same power-packed anointing as God's mandate for us. It is even more exciting when church members combine over the denominational divides that have separated us for years, to see these miracles come to pass. A very good example of such oneness in Jesus—where there could have been much dispute over doctrine and attitudes—is found in our local outreach centre, cum coffee-bar and bookshop. Open House is run and staffed by members of local Catholic and Protestant congregations of all varieties. And its very inception seemed a miracle in itself.

Four years ago our local Woodseats High Street contained an occult bookshop, The Brindled Cat, run by two well-known Sheffield witches. But local Christians, mainly unbeknown to each other, were praying against the influence of the shop in attracting young people to witches' covens. And individuals were walking round the shop claiming the property for God, and even sharing God's word, and his love, with the witches working inside. Suddenly, after a year or two, the shop closed unexpectedly, and the premises came onto the market. At this time half a dozen Christians from different churches in the area discovered they'd all been praying for The Brindled Cat to close down; so they held a special prayer-and-praise meeting, particularly to thank God that witchcraft was now much less of a threat to Woodseats, and to say, 'What next?' Maybe they almost wished they hadn't asked, because what *was* next on God's agenda seemed impossible at first to the small band of astonished Christians. They realised, as they prayed and read God's word together, and thanked him for closing down the witchcraft centre, that he seemed to be talking to them not about the premises closing but about them opening!

A fortnight later, sixteen people came together from eight local churches. They became convinced through prayer and reading God's word, particularly Isaiah 55, that God was saying 'go ahead' with claiming the corner shop and the flat above it. They knew that it should become a centre for sharing the good news, and that coffee, Christian books and cards, plus caring and counselling, would be integral to God's business there. Through tongues and interpretation and pictures that people shared in the meeting, including a whirlwind removing all obstacles in the way, faith increased until the group knew they should make an offer of £50,000 for The Brindled Cat. No one at the meeting had money to spare, but God's over-riding message was loud and clear: 'Don't look to the enormity of your need, but look to the greatness of your God.'

Three weeks later, with the £50,000 offered in faith, and accepted by the pet-shop chain vendors, a third meeting drew forty people from twelve neighbourhood churches, to hear what was happening, and to discover God's plans for his place. Slowly but surely his assorted people, from various church backgrounds, became one in seeing the same vision for what was becoming no longer The Brindled Cat but Open House instead. And it wasn't long before natural leaders started to emerge.

Ted had plenty of personnel management skill as a polytechnic careers department head. And Colin, a retired church leader, was useful in working out long-term plans. In fact, God seemed to have brought together exactly the right people to bring Open House into being. There was an accountant, Patrick, to be treasurer, an office manager, Pat, for all the secretarial skills needed (for instance in becoming a charitable trust, acquiring planning permission, and the like). A retail shop manager, Ron, found himself unemployed just at the right time to offer his valuable services. A retired doctor's receptionist, Hazel, had become a Christian recently, and her many skills included decorating the premises, along with Claudine and Brenda, who were to become the buyers for the shop, and Betty who could turn her hand to anything! Edna, though housebound then (before God healed her arthritis!) proved to be a powerful and sacrificial prayer warrior for the work—along with her friend, Marjorie. And people with pastoral, catering and teaching skills, like Robert, Val and Rosemary became involved too. And with all the practical work to be done on the premises, if there was anyone deficient at all in do-it-yourself know-how they were soon going to acquire some! (A recent addition to the attractions of Open House is the Christian video library there. It is run by Paul and Sebastian, two young men from a thriving black Pentecostal church in the city centre.)

Before any of the practicalities could come off the ground, Open House would need £5,000 to be handed over at the exchange of contracts two months later, and the further £45,000 a month after that. The time flew by, and through the first month as people caught the vision of God powerfully at work in Woodseats, money poured in for the project. Mainly it materialised as widows' mites, but together they totalled thousands of pounds. Not enough thousands though, because with only five days to go before the need to hand over £5,000 at signing of contracts, Open House was £1,500 short! An impassioned prayer meeting resulted from the realisation that most of the £3,500 had arrived during the exciting first month, but very little in the second, meaning, humanly speaking, that £1,500 seemed unobtainable in so short a time. But the Lord's word to the assembled group that night was: 'How much do you love your neighbours in Woodseats?' How far were we willing to go in faith that God would indeed supply the resources for his work? The result of that challenge was the arrangement there and then of three 6 am prayer and praise meetings spread throughout the week as a permanent fixture for the work (added to the three evening prayer meetings held each week already) and a day of fasting, finishing with a half-night of prayer fixed for three days before the contract date.

That half-night of prayer turned into a celebration meeting that could have continued all night long. And all because of a breath-taking surprise received early the morning after these new prayer meetings had been arranged. Ted received a telephone call before work from a lady of his acquaintance who knew nothing about the reason for the prayer meeting the night before, or the contract dates either, but who had heard about Open House and its future ministry. 'I've been feeling,' said the astonishing caller, 'that I should give £10,000 as a meaningful gift to the Lord, for him to use in Open House. He's told me he wants it for Open House and he wants it now.' Ted could have fallen through the floor—or rather jumped through the rafters for joy! With that amazing answer to prayer God had given a glorious seal that his people were hearing his plans for his place. By the time the completion date arrived the whole £50,000 was ready to hand over, with many more sacrificial gifts from the Lord's people, and a substantial loan from the bank. The loan might have seemed less than God's perfect provision but for the fact that each month the £500 needed to be paid out by Open House for all the overheads continued to materialise. Many times God's people at Open House have been reminded of the fact that we aren't to look to the size of the bills but to the greatness of our God. And because he's providing for what is his business, the staff he sends can afford continually to be about his business of caring and counselling, without a moment being spent in raising funds.

'Glory to God in the highest,' everyone sang that first Christmas at the Open House carol service. Somebody noticed that crossing out the 'e' in 'highest' (maybe standing for crossing out the exchequer!) leaves, 'Glory to God in the High St.' And certainly that's the purpose of Open House, as a steady stream of people in need continue to discover. People in physical need—like the lady crippled so badly with arthritis that her fingers weren't even able to turn the taps or fasten buttons. Nessie's husband was her help-meet in every way, and her security too, but he was needing to go into hospital for surgery for a fortnight when they called at Open House for a tearful cup of tea, a day or two before his departure. Claudine (Ted's wife) and her friend Brenda were the two café staff on duty that morning. (Open House is completely staffed and run by volunteers.) Talking to their sorrowful customers they discovered Nessie's sad predicament and found she'd like them to pray with her—but upstairs in the counselling room where it would be more private. Brenda and Claudine were glad it was more private, too, because they were both beginners in praying aloud for healing and felt totally incompetent. It took a terribly long time for arthritic Nessie to ascend those stairs, but five minutes later she sailed down them like a new woman. As well she might, because she was! And her husband felt almost as good as if he'd been healed too!

Many people in spiritual need have been helped to see light in their darkness too—and sometimes to move permanently into the light, like Harry, the elderly gentleman of seventy-nine, who discovered what he'd been looking for all his life in Open House, and celebrated by being baptised by full immersion, despite his health indicating he shouldn't risk it. And now he helps out in an old people's home with all the exuberance of a young believer—which he is!

Social needs have also often been met through the friendship of Open House with volunteers like Jim and Eileen serving the Lord's loving care along with the tea and scones. And through people loving their neighbours in practical ways—like an ex-merchant seaman discovered when he came into the café for help with his complicated Giro forms. Through those forms being filled in he soon met Jesus and began a new life with him some weeks later. But first he met the love of his life behind the counter in the form of a lady called Heather. All of that came about because, after Shirley had successfully helped Mike with those Giro forms, he returned to thank her but mistook Heather for Shirley—a mistake that led to love at first sight for them both. Shortly afterwards, Heather was the recipient of a miracle that opened Mike's eyes to God's power for the first time.

Heather bakes the weekly supply of scones for Open House, but a day or two after Mike had first met her she arrived for work on crutches, due to slipping down a step in the dark on her way to an early morning prayer meeting that day. The hospital told her she'd torn a ligament and wouldn't be able to walk for three weeks. But Heather had to because, as well as baking for Open House, she was also looking after our neighbour, Maureen, through a particularly crippling phase of Parkinson's disease. Their both being on crutches was no good at all, of course, so we'd prayed next-door at our Tuesday fellowship that morning for a miracle for Heather. And as Heather faithfully started out for her baking stint at Open House that lunchtime, she suddenly knew she didn't need her crutches any more. She was totally healed, to the faith-creating amazement of her new young man.

Experiencing miracles seems to be part of God's mandate for Open House. Monday night was Young People's night for a long time, giving youngsters on the streets somewhere to go. Somewhere to meet people with time to listen and to care, and to share too. Particularly to share God's answers for youngsters in trouble, of any sort. One basically simple but desperate trouble was answered through Ted's faith-filled prayer one night. A young man called Steve had hurt his hand badly when he swung a mighty punch during a fight. His opponent had ducked and Steve's hand had crashed heavily into a lamppost, leaving it swollen and immobilised. He was due to go to a long-awaited interview with the Marines the next day, where he would have to prove his physical fitness on a now-impossible assault course. But Ted prayed and the hand was so totally healed that Steve came out top of all the applicants on the course that weekend!

Of course, plenty of the young people still seem

unimpressed by Open House's message, as Roy and Pauline who began the work can testify; and so too are many daytime visitors. But who can tell what seeds might be secretly taking root? Sometimes people say things like, 'It was your smile that suddenly had me know Jesus must care about me too, and started me on my way to him.' And then we know that whatever discouragements the enemy of our souls might send to try and make us give up, he's only worried because of the invisible harvest coming to fruition.

Sometimes Satan tries extra hard, especially when he sees the sacrificial love he detests so much being put into practice. He particularly tries to use differences of tradition in worship to separate us, so it's especially good for Open House staff and friends to meet regularly in free and faith-filled worship together. Any differences are quickly forgotten as God's people praise together, set free from being a 'holy huddle' by a common desire to reach a dying world with God's good news. And sometimes God uses the fellowship to bless visitors just as much as the regulars.

That's what happened when our friends Sue and Dave and their little children arrived back from a year with Mission Aviation Fellowship in Western Australia, where David trained to be a pilot in an outback situation. They were both absolutely exhausted and feeling at a spiritual all-time low from much satanic opposition and oppression over there, although they were meant to be training for the African mission-field. That night our evening house-fellowship meeting was moving, en masse, to join Open House's more formal worship and planning meeting—particularly so we could provide the musicians they were short of. 'What a shame,' I thought before we left. 'If we were meeting here then both Sue and Dave could stay to the meeting while the children slept upstairs. And even though Dave can come with us to the Open House meeting, it'll be more formal than ours, and Dave won't be able to share his troubles. And he certainly looks as if he needs to.'

It really was a case of loving our neighbours enough to supply their needs when we'd said 'yes' in the first place to missing our meeting for theirs. So many blessings had resulted from the get-togethers at our house that it was hard to forego even one of them. But God has good reasons for not allowing us to get into a rut—even a seemingly good one—as he made apparent that evening.

We were halfway through the scheduled order for the Open House meeting when Katey, a sixth former from our group, recently converted and rather timid, said, 'I'm sure God wants to heal people here.' The chairman thanked her for her comment, adding that he was sure she was right, then continued with the programme. But I knew Katey was more than right; that to have said anything about it at all she must be feeling God's anointing upon her to pray for someone specifically.

I'd been ferrying people to the meeting until after it had begun, and there was just one seat left for me when I finally arrived, fortuitously next to Dave. So now I knew to whisper to him, 'Dave, do you feel you might like prayer for your heartache to be healed?' He nodded. So when brave Katey broke in again after the next song, to repeat that someone might still need healing because she knew she should be praying that way, I was immediately able to nudge Dave. And though his distress was basically spiritual, not physical, he did have a knee injury too, to extend the scope of Katey's prayers. A minute later Katey was kneeling in front of Dave praying in silence while I spoke out words of healing and renewal for him. They were quickly interrupted though by someone else wailing out heart-rending, primitive-sounding sobs. I wondered whether some occult Aboriginal influence was releasing Dave as those wails continued. And from the smile that slowly broke upon his face, turning into a radiant beam for everyone, we knew that some transforming spiritual transaction we didn't understand had definitely taken place—as it soon would for Sue, through her renewed husband returning home to pray for her.

But we understood even less what took place next! As Dave rose to go, deciding he'd walk home to test his prayed-over knee, an elderly gentleman, Ron, said he was going the same way. But he'd been lame for years, so he said he knew he couldn't possibly keep up with Dave. 'Come on, try,' Dave urged Ron. And to their astonishment as Ron strode out increasingly powerfully at Dave's side, they discovered it was Ron's leg and not Dave's that had been healed. Ron was so wonderfully healed that he could run for buses again, after many years of shuffling along with no hope. On a Monday night he went along to Open House to tell all the 'wild' teenagers his wonderful story.

God certainly does move in mysterious ways, but as long as his wonders continue to be performed as a result, we're happy to continue sharing our lives together, warts and all, wherever he might lead—and especially on our high streets for him!

12
Food for Thought

The church—the 'living stones' variety, not the building—is the one institution where the members should be good at being gregarious and getting on with each other. And God makes it very clear in his word that we're meant to be each other's servants so that the world will know we're Christians by our love (John 13:35). He wants to change us to be so much like Jesus that we're able to suffer even the most garrulous, irritating or conceited of Christians gladly for his sake—while *he* changes them!

Instead, as the world looks at the church, it can often see back-biting, holy huddles and power-seeking, along with the poor, handicapped, maladjusted or lonely members being ignored. 'Help to carry one another's burdens,' we're exhorted (Galatians 6:2). And that command applies especially to church life. For one thing, the world is meant to look at us and say, 'See how those Christians love one another!'—not to notice how fast we can leave a church when the members don't suit us. (Sometimes, of course, the Almighty can direct us to join a different church because he wants to use us in a new way.)

For another thing, human beings were never designed to bear life's burdens alone. Burdens should always be shared with the Lord, of course, but he often wants to use other people to help us take the strain too. That's why we mustn't allow touchiness, bitterness or unforgiveness to get in the way of fellowship with each other—or jealousy either. Because burdens can break us if we aren't willing to let others share the load—and particularly the burden of loneliness. So we've trained our children as well as ourselves in cheering up the lonely people others might not notice.

'Mum, I've just been asking the grown-ups who live on their own to come for dinner,' beamed John, rushing up to me at the end of the Sunday morning service, with a column of uncertain-looking people in tow. 'Here's Richard, and Miss Johnson, and Bill, and Ada, and they'd all like to come. You're glad, aren't you? Because our Sunday School teacher said we had to think of something nice to cheer up lonely people who live on their own.' John looked very pleased with himself as I tried to appear delighted, thinking of Grandpa and Aunty Edna with us for the weekend, as well as my mother and her elderly friend, Molly, and two of the teenagers' friends, all needing dinner. But I couldn't have managed it too well because everyone, except half-starved Richard, suddenly had urgent reasons for having to go home!

Actually, like John, I'm very much a 'more the merrier' type of person, but the rest of the adult household definitely weren't just then, and sometimes, being a good neighbour to your nearest and dearest means not seeming to be a very good neighbour to your neighbour! The very thought of our family's collective faces when

the already overcrowded table became jammed with
colliding elbows, as everyone endeavoured to enjoy their
square-inch of Sunday roast was just too much for me.
But maybe if I'd known then about my faith-filled
neighbour in the church, Gladys, I'd have braved the
black looks in case God had similar plans in mind for
me.

Gladys' miracle began when she had a phone call one
Saturday night from her sister up in North Yorkshire.
'Hello, Gladys,' she said. 'We thought we'd come over to
see you for the day tomorrow. That's all right, isn't it?'
she added, confidently, as only sisters can. 'Oh yes, that's
lovely,' replied Gladys, secretly wondering how she was
going to make the meat go round, as she and her
husband Les had invited a new friend from church for
dinner the next day. And when she had another look at
the small joint she'd splashed out on that morning,
barely big enough for the three of them, she knew it was
impossible. She might scrape enough money together
for sausages to stretch the meat a bit further, but it was
too late to go to the shops by then, anyway. And even
though the little grocer's shop opposite opened on
Sundays, there was no way Gladys could spoil the Lord's
day by shopping on it. If only her relatives didn't have
such hearty northern appetites. But they did, so that was
that.

The next morning Gladys peeled a bumper bowlful of
potatoes. And when it became time to serve the meal she
made sure their visitors' line of vision was filled with
such a massive bowl of mashed potatoes that they might
overlook the sight of Les carving that miniscule joint.
She'd whispered to him in the kitchen as the guests were
sitting down, 'Carve it as thin as you can, Les, and pray

for each piece to be extra filling, too!' Both Les and Gladys came from a Pentecostal background, and were used to praying for everything under the sun, but I doubt whether they'd ever prayed for a joint of beef before! So Les silently offered each slice to the Lord as he carved away, and it slowly dawned on him that the joint wasn't shrinking as it should have been.

Soon all five of them had a very respectable plate of meat, and were tucking into Gladys' fine Yorkshire puddings and accompaniments with relish. And they didn't need any Yorkshire Relish, either, to help down the delicious beef—so delicious that everyone enjoyed second helpings! Les and Gladys grinned at each other incredulously across the table, noticing they'd still not finished their miracle joint. So next day Les enjoyed the last of the meat in well-filled sandwiches for work. And Gladys praised God that 'keeping Sunday special' meant she'd gained so much more than the sausages she might have acquired to supplement the meat. Particularly the gain of knowing Philippians 4:19 even applies to such mundane items as Sunday lunch, when putting God first and loving our neighbours are our main priorities.

Loving our neighbours in church life can also sometimes mean putting ourselves out on a limb for them spiritually. A lot of us find no trouble in being hospitable, or taking on sick-visiting, or even lending our car, say to a brother or sister in need. And some of our church members have stayed up all night with people who are really ill. But even the most taxing practical tasks can seem no trouble at all compared with daring to pray out loud, for instance, with someone in need—particularly when it has to be over the telephone. Or seeming to push ourselves forward in speaking out in the service at a relevant moment, when most people think we're meant to leave all that to the minister. And sometimes playing any part in ministry when we're new Christians can seem impertinent when some church members have been around for so much longer.

But, of course, the enemy of our souls delights to use all those irrelevancies to paralyse us into uselessness. And we often need to remember that loving our neighbour, in or out of church, means ignoring what other people might think. Like the day I had a hard battle taking a smelly, alcoholic tramp home for tea. He seemed to be showing a desire to change his life as I talked to him at the end of a nearby gospel open-air meeting, and the Lord nudged me that he needed to see love in action. We'd some well-to-do church friends coming for tea, and I tried to convince myself that he was just like all the other seemingly hopeless 'ne'er do wells' I'd met who weren't willing for change. I knew how our friends might scoff, inwardly at least, at my naive, do-gooding nature. Neil's obvious need won the day though and he was soon tucking the tea away at our well-filled table, seated as far away from our friends as I could arrange.

He disappeared from our lives a few weeks later and I'll probably never discover the lasting results, if any, of that embarrassing tea-time. But at least I knew Neil's heart had been warmed, and the rest of him too, that very cold day; and that Stephanie and John, beneath the age of minding a bit of muck, had found him a most amusing guest, with his fund of childhood jokes!

Kind Steffie was working out which bed he should sleep in when I thankfully discovered he was expected back at the Salvation Army hostel. So it was good to know he could continue to be looked after, body, soul and spirit, there—and especially the latter, as he gave up the wrong sort of spirit, and all alcohol, before his damaged liver got the better of him.

Sometimes we need to keep on helping and hoping, as we pray and work in the church without seeing much reward for our labours; but occasionally the Lord plans an immediate miraculous surprise, as we make ourselves available to be about his business, not our own, helping people in need. Just as long as we're willing to take risks for him, and each other—as Gordon taught me a few years ago now.

Gordon was starting to attend an Anglican church situated alongside Sheffield United's football stadium, where Billy Graham had been 'packing them in' for a week in the summer of 1985. That's where Gordon had met Jesus in a powerful way.

And although, after a while, he'd drifted from his previous church, some Christian friends had been used by God to heal his chronic depression, so he'd decided to attend the nearest church to his home in thanksgiving. He'd enjoyed the service and had come back to praise the Lord there a second time; and that's when God started to teach Gordon that obedience often seems to be spelled r-i-s-k.

The service that Sunday morning provided an opportunity for thanksgiving for more of the congregation than just Gordon. Win and Victor had been married forty-five years, and it was a miracle in more ways than one that unbelieving Victor was there in the service at all. A few weeks earlier he'd told Win she could have whatever she liked for an anniversary present. But Win wanted only one thing—'For you to come to church with me, Victor, to celebrate our wedding anniversary there!' Win had faithfully attended church for forty years, continually praying for her husband. But the nearest Victor had ever come to a church service had been walking Win to St Mary's on Christmas and New Year's Eve, and returning to walk her back home again as the late-night services finished. And Victor had an added reason to refuse Win's request.

For years Victor had suffered increasingly agonising arthritis, and now at sixty-nine he was in constant torment from it. After a lifetime labouring in the heat of Sheffield's steel works, where he sweated so copiously that his clothes rotted on his back, this tall, well-built man now spent most of his time lying on his bed, with a foam-covered board placed on top of the mattress. The thought of shuffling into church on his crutches and enduring being seated through a service was almost too much—especially when he didn't believe in God. But he'd told Win she could have her heart's desire, and being a man of his word he made sure she did. The celebration service was a family affair, so he had a painful lift to the church in one of their children's cars. But once inside the church they found the polished Victorian pews were too narrow for Victor's broad frame, and Maureen, the deaconess taking the service, arranged for the bishop's chair to be placed next to Win's pew-end.

All through the service Win was suffering so much for Victor, in even more agony than usual in his seated position, that it was hard to remember it was a celebration service. Maureen prayed for God's healing power for both Victor and Win, as Win had suffered a heart attack a while before, so had to be very careful to take things easy. And somehow, with true Yorkshire grit, Victor managed to stay seated, sticking it out until the end of the sacrificial service. So it must have been extra hard when a minute or two after the service had finished Gordon approached him. He was so desperate to be back home on his board again.

Gordon had been feeling more and more nervous as the service drew to a close, because he was more and more aware that he was meant to go over and pray for Victor and Win. And even though the minister had already prayed for them God didn't remove the conviction. So he forced himself through the well-wishers, and told the celebration couple, 'I think I'm meant to . . . er . . . pray for you both . . . if you don't mind.' His few halting words in English for God's healing power to descend soon turned into a fluent flow in tongues, Gordon's heavenly prayer language. Victor's born-again son-in-law, Bob, was sitting just along the pew from Win, and suddenly he surprised himself and everyone else by breaking into Gordon's prayer. 'He's healed,' he exclaimed. 'I just felt the power go through my legs!'

Win could hardly take it in as she busied herself taking everyone a piece of the special celebration cake she'd brought to go with the church coffee. But when Victor left the church a quarter of an hour later without his crutches, and spent the rest of the day away from his bed, she knew for a fact that Bob was right. Victor was healed, without a shadow of doubt. *Ransomed, restored and delivered, too*, thought Win, gazing at her now faith-filled husband. But it wasn't until the next Friday that Win discovered there was still one comparatively small shadow for Victor that he was trying hard to understand.

It was as they were preparing to visit their daughter and her family to show them, rather than tell them, the wonderful news about Grandpa. 'This is the strange thing,' Victor confided in Win, as she searched for the telephone number for the taxi. 'The Lord's taken away every vestige of pain from my body except from my knees.' And as Victor stood gazing at those recalcitrant knees, Win suddenly understood what Victor had to do.

'You know, love,' she smiled, 'when God healed you in church it was a total surprise. You never even asked for it. And I think he's left your knees out so that you've something left to ask him for yourself. You see, he loves his children to ask for what they need.' So Victor did, and by the time the taxi arrived he was happily rejoicing in a new pair of knees, too!

Like the rest of his joints, they were going to remain completely painless for the rest of his life. And it was almost as if Victor knew he'd only ten months to live for his mighty, mind-blowing Lord, here on planet earth. Everywhere he went, at bus-stops, in shops, at Christian meetings and anywhere else there was opportunity, he delighted in telling people how Jesus had met his every need, and could meet theirs too. So when he suddenly found himself face to face with his beloved Lord, with an unexpected internal haemorrhage supplying his marching orders, Win knew Victor would have no regrets.

She, of course, being left behind with her bad heart, had a few. But she's steadily found Jesus to be more and more the supplier of her heart's need, and every other need as well. And every time she needs a special lift she

can just look across to her sideboard and see the photo
of herself and her poor, pained husband, about to enter
St Mary's Church that anniversary morning—and then
look across to the photos taken a month later. There's
Victor standing tall and erect, ready for wherever the
good fight of faith might lead. And with names like
theirs, it's extra appropriate that they should both have
discovered so brilliantly how to be 'more than
conquerors'—together and, briefly, apart!

WORK-OUT 4
Neighbours in the Church

As thorough an Englishman as ever coveted his neighbours' goods.

(Charles Kingsley, 1819–75)

Who gives himself, with his alms, feeds three. Himself, his hungering neighbour, and Me.

(James Lovell, 1819–91)

1. CHURCHGOERS CAN'T BE CHOOSY
Whatever might be happening with the orthodox structures of denominational fences, a grass-roots growing together of Christians of all denominations is spreading fast, particularly through increasing city-wide rallies for evangelism and renewal, and through praise marches.
Read 1 John 4:7–22.

(a) How many denominations do we feel at home with?
(b) How possible does it seem to us that the ecumenical movement will one day see divisive denominational structures demolished for unity?
(c) Would we be willing to change denominations if moving house, or the like, gave us the choice of travelling back to our old church or joining local Christians in a different denomination? Are house churches a denomination now?
(d) How often do we worship with people from other denominations?

2. OPEN HOUSE—OPEN HEARTS
Read 1 Thessalonians 5:12–28.

(a) 'The church that prays together stays together.' Why is the prayer meeting often the most poorly attended meeting for many churches? What can we do about it?

(b) Has your church or fellowship ever held a day of prayer and fasting to hear God's voice on a particular matter? Should that happen, in the light of Jesus saying, 'When you fast'—not 'If you fast' (Matthew 6:16)?

(c) How far can we disagree with our pastor/minister/house-group leader while continuing to obey 1 Thessalonians 5:12–13?

(d) What are the conditions for hearing God's voice, individually and as a body?

3. FOOD FOR THOUGHT
Read Acts 2:43–47.

(a) Do we believe that every miracle Jesus performed he can do through us today—from food-multiplying to raising the dead (John 14:12)?

(b) What do you think were the main reasons for Victor's healing happening when it did?

(c) Which has most impact in evangelism: inspired preaching, loving lives, or signs and wonders? What influenced *you* the most in turning to Christ?

(d) How can we as individuals best help our local church body become strong in caring for each other, and for the practical, emotional and spiritual needs of our non-Christian neighbours?

Praise Point: 'He who calls you will do it, because he is faithful' (1 Thessalonians 5:24).

PART FIVE
Neighbours in the Community

13

Give and Take

Any minute now the doorbell is going to ring, I thought dismally. It was almost time for the weekly fellowship meeting held in our front room, but as our ancient Hoover suddenly blew out its contents around the carpet and then died on me, it looked as if we'd be meeting in the kitchen instead. At least we'd be handy for the coffee! Then, as I gathered up the grey fluff, the phone rang simultaneously with little Steffie knocking the neatly folded pile of ironing from the top of the stairs to the bottom. I was right about the doorbell too.

On the other side of the door stood an attractive, very cool, calm and collected young lady from down the road. I knew her by sight as a member of our local house church, and by now we'd become used to people of all denominations (and none) arriving for the fellowship. *What a lovely surprise! Sue's come for the meeting*, I decided. *But did it have to be just when the house and I are looking such a sight?* was my next self-centred thought. *Sue would never guess it isn't usually a slum from the way it looks just now.* But I was wrong about Sue's reason for coming. She wasn't there for the meeting at all, but to bring a

167

message from her church. However, as she stood in the hall, she got the message about me even before she'd delivered hers—particularly as she saw the mess, and little Stephanie making it even messier. Then, as the phone rang again, and the gate clicked open behind her with the first arrivals for the meeting, Sue had a very kind thought.

'You really could do with a bit of help on Tuesday mornings,' she smiled encouragingly. 'My mother's looking after the little ones next Tuesday, you know, so I could come up early and help you get straight before the meeting, if you like.' *How wonderfully caring*, I thought, *especially as Sue doesn't even know me. And what a good illustration of Christians being sisters from the moment they meet, that she can instantly be such a good Samaritan.* I only had one qualm: what on earth would Sue think of our house? I couldn't help suspecting that hers would look like something straight out of the Ideal Home Exhibition.

And that's why, the next Tuesday, I was doubly worried. If only it weren't the long-neglected upstairs toilet and bathroom that claimed Sue's conscientious attention. They'd been needing redecorating for ages, and had somehow missed out on the spring cleaning too. But I had no choice in the matter when I suggested her tackling such a challenge. The trouble was I'd forgotten that Matthew and Elinor were on holiday from their secondary school that week.

Being off school on a Tuesday morning means their becoming a more or less willing workforce to see the house cleaned and prepared for the meeting in half the usual time. And we'd just finished our tasks, forgetting all about Sue, when she rang the bell, ready for work.

My mind went into a flat spin. She was such a wonderful neighbour that she'd even brought her apron and cleaning implements with her so that she wouldn't have to keep interrupting my work to ask the whereabouts of my dusters and brushes. 'Oh Lord,' I thought, arrowing the need to him, 'please forgive my amnesia, and show me what Sue can do.' And right on target the thought of those messy upstairs rooms came to mind.

And they really were messy, because it was a good half-hour before Sue came downstairs again, with the satisfaction of a job well done. So I was delighted that she had time for a well-earned coffee, and to stay for part of the meeting too after such an exhausting task. I soon forgot my shameful housewifery as the meeting progressed and our attention centred on Jesus instead of on ourselves—particularly helped by Pat, our brilliant pianist, who causes the piano keys to open locked doors in our hearts to the Lord. And suddenly it came into my mind that during the preceding week it had seemed the Lord was leading me to expect people to be healed when we were next praising God together, as a natural result of 'the Lord inhabiting the praises of his people'; and particularly that I should have faith for at least one person to know the joy of physical healing through prayer in Jesus' name, there and then. So, at a convenient point, I whispered to Audrey, who was leading the meeting that morning, 'I've a feeling that somehow the Lord's wanting to heal someone of something!' Audrey shared my impression with everyone, while I hoped I'd heard the Lord aright. But I'd prayed a minute before that God would give me a gap in the meeting in order to pass the message on if it were from him—so now I had to trust his sovereignty.

It was hard, though, because everyone sat in silence, and nobody moved towards the lonely prayer-chair someone had placed in the centre of the room. It looked as if no one would, either, despite the number of elderly ladies who were there that morning. But suddenly a new voice startled us all. It was Sue saying she was sure she must be the one. We all looked at her in amazement. She seemed the youngest and fittest among us! 'The trouble is,' she explained, 'I've been suffering increasingly from bad vertigo for the last few months. So bad that it can even come upon me when I'm driving the car, and render me totally incapable for ages with a blinding headache, sickness and impossible dizziness. Especially impossible with three little children to look after.'

Poor Sue, I thought. *However has she coped all this time? And who'd have thought, to look at her beautiful smile, that she had a care in the world!* At the same time I was really thrilled that Sue could stay to get healed—she certainly deserved it after all that cleaning. It would be a lovely present from the Lord for such a kind person. Then I started to wonder whom he'd lead to pray for Sue.

By now Sue was sitting in that low prayer-chair in the centre of the room. (It was my mother's old baby-nursing chair; at just the right height for laying-on of hands, as well as for feeding babies—a good reminder that we're all King's kids, in constant need of heavenly sustenance.) I sat back, thinking I'd done my bit in opening the way for Sue's healing, and that now one of the people particularly involved in the healing ministry could move into the centre to pray. But I was disappointed, and worried too, because no one moved a muscle, even though I stared hard at one or two people I thought would be willing. Praying for healing for people just wasn't my scene, but I was increasingly aware that Sue could well be feeling herself to be some sort of social leper, with nobody at all wanting to join her in that lonely centre of our circle. *Oh Lord* I thought despairingly half a minute later as I forced myself to walk forward to my solitary sister, *you know this is a waste of time. And so will everyone else. Why didn't you nudge one of the experts a bit harder? I've no idea how to pray for Sue.* And just to let anyone who happened to be looking know how clueless I was, I only placed one hand on Sue's head, instead of the then more customary two for laying-on of hands.

Feeling desperate, I opened my mouth in faith and found myself saying, 'Thank you, God, for your healing for Sue.' And then I surprised myself even more by praying a long prayer for her family, and for God's perfect plans for the years to come. Suddenly I ran out of words, said 'Amen', and sat back in my place. I thought that it might have seemed a funny prayer and hoped that Sue didn't feel too let down.

Then we sang again, and Sue had to go. As she left she stopped and whispered in my ear, 'Hilary, when you were praying just then you did only place *one* hand on my head, didn't you? Because I suddenly felt two hands, and it was as if they were turning my brain round in the opposite direction to the way it spins when the vertigo begins. And then the hands let my brain settle back to normal, like a pendulum. So they must have been the Lord's hands. But I'll wait for three months before I tell anyone whether I'm healed or not, just to be sure.' I stared at Sue, staggered, as she smiled her goodbyes to those in the meeting, still singing their praises to God for all his power, whether Sue had felt it or not. But I was beginning to feel she surely had, even though it was too soon to share the evidence.

Or was it? Because that afternoon I needed to go down to the infant school gate to collect John from his day's play. And as I stood chatting to the other parents there, we were joined by Ann, a faith-filled young mum who'd been at the meeting that morning. She isn't shy of letting others know that Jesus is alive, so she came straight out with her breathtaking news.

'You know this morning,' she said, 'when you prayed for that new young woman with vertigo? Well, I suddenly felt I should open my eyes, and when I did I could hardly believe it. Because there was Jesus standing at the side of her, with both of his hands on her head. And he looked so beautiful, and I just knew he was healing her. So I thought you might like to tell her, if you know where she lives.'

'I can't wait,' I reassured Ann. And all the way up to Sue's, walking slowly hand-in-hand with our dawdling son, I couldn't get over the wonder of Jesus standing there in our most unideal home. There at the side of our scruffy, chipped kitchen chair, blessing my new sister Sue—almost beyond belief! I thanked God from the bottom of my heart for sending her, not only to be healed, but to help me to be healed too, of caring what other people think. And to teach me to be willing to be helped, even when it involves someone seeing my flaws, or my floors, as the case may be!

I'm pleased to say that I'm almost as healed of my need to impress people as Sue is of her vertigo—which is saying a lot, because since that day five years ago Sue has not had another attack of vertigo. One of the joys of being part of a caring and praying group is being enabled more and more to have nothing to hide. And discovering that, fashionable or frumpy, free and easy or fastidious, we all have areas in our minds, emotions and wills—as well as in our bodies—that need healing. As together we're seeking for Jesus to come first in our lives, it's exciting to see all the ways he can bring about that healing, and use us for others—maybe next-door, or maybe halfway round the world, through prayer and giving, and loving whoever he sends. Sometimes, like Sue, the new neighbours he gives us are wonderfully easy to love and appreciate, but sometimes they're not. As we keep ignoring our natural likes and dislikes every time his supernatural love is called for, we'll find that appreciating each other can come more and more naturally—as Dave, our young next-door neighbour, discovered one Tuesday in the meeting.

Dave had grown up feeling very rejected and thoroughly against society, not knowing the love of parents, and finding even the best care of his children's home inadequate. He was finding it very hard to like anyone at all, when he met Jesus and discovered the love he'd always lacked. And gradually over the years, he'd learned to care more and more for a very small but slowly increasing number of people. So I had a real surprise at the end of one of the meetings when Dave confided in me, 'Hilary, I don't know how to cope with this, because during the meeting I suddenly felt my eyes fill with tears for everyone in the room. I could feel a strange sort of affectionate, caring love for everyone that I knew must be God's love, but half the people there I still don't even like!' He looked at me seriously. 'Just how do I cope with feeling that way about people I can't even *begin* to like?'

'Well, I'd just enjoy it if I were you,' I said. 'The only coping I have difficulty with is when God doesn't give me any good feeling at all about someone I dislike, and then says, "Right—go and do them good with a hug, or a bit of baking, or offering to play tennis with them, or whatever!" And there's only one way I can accept people I can't stand, just as they are, without having to change them. It's to remember that God accepts my very messy self just as I am—without wanting to change me till I'm ready for it. And the more I accept them, the more able I seem to share God's love for the person too.'

Of course it's true that God loves us just as we are, but loves us too much to let us stay as we are. And he wants that uncomfortable transforming love to flow through us to others too. Sometimes it flows through our example to people in a mess. Those people need to see a good role-model of living God's way so they can be inspired to live likewise, and begin to move out of that mess. Sometimes, when the people we're wanting to help know they can trust us and that we have their best interests at heart, it's safe to share how obvious shortcomings can be eliminated, when we can tell it's the right moment for maximum impact with minimum offence.

That's how it was with Wayne, the teenager from the homeless men's hostel down the road. He'd grown up abused and rejected, and then unhappy in less-than-adequate foster homes. He was desperate for friendship and acceptance, and really wanted to help people too. 'The trouble is, nobody wants me,' he said. 'Even when I visit old ladies to cheer them up they won't answer the door the next time I go.' I could see Wayne really wanted to know how to find friends and become acceptable in society. The trouble was, he had a voice like a foghorn and he'd never learned to moderate it. So I told him, and helped him practise being 'sweet and low'. And we all came to an agreement that we'd tell him every time his voice began to blast us out.

I also needed to tell him every time he started to follow me around like a lost duckling fixated on the nearest mother hen! It made me feel anything but protective to have Wayne's large, ungainly figure looming six inches behind me like an overgrown shadow with every step I took, as I cleaned the house, or answered the door, or cooked the dinner. Of course I let him help me with the housework but his concentration span was two minutes at the most, and he quickly reverted to being my security-chasing shadow. No wonder that even lonely old ladies had found Wayne's visits too wearing—especially as he never cleaned his teeth, his clothes, or anything else, at first! But soon Wayne was becoming more and more a social asset, as he learned to be clean, tidy and sweet-smelling. And he found drugs and cigarettes weren't what he needed any more—even though he kept slipping back into taking them. Slowly his essentially helpful, caring nature was able to emerge unhindered in God's divine give-and-take system.

We're especially aided in helping 'problem people' by our next-door neighbours. 'For Sale' signs in our neighbourhood become family prayer projects, as we ask God to send either new neighbours who are willing to meet him, or ones who know him already. He did the latter with the houses on either side of us, and sent Barry and Beryl, and Keith and Maureen. They're definitely neighbours for whom Jesus comes first—Keith and

Maureen's house containing four bedsits for anyone in need, and Beryl being a brilliant Bible teacher for our Thursday morning study.

There have been lots of other Waynes for David and myself—and our neighbours—and we've always found that people have been willing to respond to God's love and discipline through the friends he sends, 'give and take' has summed up the results on both sides. Giving constant caring discipline does cost a lot, but there is always plenty of 'taking' too. Taking satisfaction in seeing God breaking old habit patterns that have kept lives once full of promise in chains. And sometimes taking sorrow and heartbreak when people decide, maybe temporarily, that it's easier slipping back into their chains. But the best taking, for us and the person involved too, is taking heart. Taking heart that God is able to do all that he promises and more for any life, in whatever state, just as long as we're willing to give and take, totally, his way.

14

Team Support

By now I must have read almost every book available on sharing the good news, and they've all left me feeling the same way—worn out. And that's before I start sharing! There are so many different methods, pitfalls, Bible verses to learn and evangelical events to organise, that the very best plan seems to be to leave it all to the experts.

When I remember, however, that the real expert is the Holy Spirit, and that I'm a Holy Spirit container, I can see how his programming can make even me an evangelist. All the books make sense when I know that God can guide me into any of the right methods for all the right moments. Basically, successful evangelism is just being the right person at the right time, in the right place with the right message—whether the message is conveyed by word, deed, or sometimes just an expression.

Those stickers saying, 'Smile, Jesus loves you,' might seem simplistic, as if a smile is the answer to all our problems, but a smile for the right person at just the right time can be life-changing—as I discovered one dismal murky morning.

I must have been very bleary-eyed as I walked down to school with our tribe and one or two others, because I thought the stranger with two children in tow was someone else. And I beamed at her before I realised she wasn't. But I beamed long enough for her to look at me and think, 'Well, if she can look happy with that lot, maybe I can cope somehow. She was new to the district, I discovered, as we began to talk. She was feeling very lonely, as well as being desperate about managing her children. But that chance smile led to a conversation that brought her to our house for the next Tuesday fellowship, and before long she too had plenty to smile about.

Smiles need to be part of all the means God gives for sharing his good news. Particularly at open-air meetings, where unsmiling saints make passers-by think, 'No thanks, I've enough troubles of my own.' But joy on the faces of the believers could initiate the thought, 'I might be missing something,' even for people who don't catch the words being spoken or sung there.

Another way we can get out with the gospel is through door-to-door visitation. If only we knew behind which doors were the people ready to think and talk about a living faith, our work would be a lot easier. Occasionally, of course, God will guide us in a supernatural way to a certain house where he knows there's great need. But more often he'll put an area in our hearts, especially in our church neighbourhood, to visit systematically door to door as a fellowship. That's what happened with our next-door neighbour's home-help and the church she belonged to. They followed the Lord's instructions to go out in twos, but Kathleen's partner was ill one cold, blustery day and had to stay at home. Kathleen, knowing how many houses there were to visit, felt she must carry on anyway, even though almost every door she called at that afternoon seemed to give her the cold shoulder. She was covering a new block of flats, but by the time she reached the top floor she felt so cold, tired and discouraged that she was very tempted just to push the rest of her leaflets through the doors without knocking. But as she walked towards the first door of that freezing top floor she had her mind changed.

'What if Jesus had decided he couldn't quite cope with enduring to the end?' came into her head, and she realised she could 'endure' too for the sake of anyone on the other side of those doors who might otherwise never hear about Jesus first hand. But, at the same time, she couldn't help hoping everyone was out! At the third door, after yet more rejection, there seemed—at last—to be nobody in. But just as Kathleen started to move away, she heard what seemed to be a sob on the other side of the door. So she knocked again. The door opened a crack, and a breaking voice whispered, 'Yes, what is it?' As Kathleen explained why she'd come she noticed a row of half-full pill bottles lined up behind the tearful lady. 'You know, Jesus can cope,' she encouraged her, 'however much we can't.' At that Kathleen was ushered in and the lady broke down and told her all. 'My life is just so meaningless and lonely and miserable,' she wept. 'I was just about to take these pills.'

As Kathleen silently praised God that she'd bothered to knock, she explained to Rose that if we're wanting to die anyway, we might as well do it the Jesus way, and give our life away instead, to him. And then, as she explained how Jesus had already given his life away to rescue us, Rose's tears stopped and her eyes filled with hope. Soon the hope turned to joy as she prayed the sinner's prayer with Kathleen and knew she'd begun a brand new life. No wonder the enemy had so desperately tried to discourage Kathleen from completing her task, knowing what could be about to happen behind Rose's door. But he completely lost the battle, because Rose was very soon helping to introduce others to Jesus—and delighting everyone with her lovely piano playing for the local Sunday School.

Most evangelism happens, though, without any organisation at all, as friends 'gossip the gospel'—and quite often without being aware of it. Sometimes Jesus badges can be the means of a powerful silent witness, especially when the wearer is consistently cheerful and helpful. One friend who realised she'd been given too much change by her local newsagent after she'd left the shop, went back to return the extra £1, and found that the Jesus sticker on her jacket led her into a really useful conversation with the newsagent, who was impressed by her honesty. Eventually, after lots of ups and downs, it led to him and his family becoming part of the local church family. But it's good advice to make sure you're free from besetting sins, like bad temper (or bad breath!) before you proclaim you're a Jesus person by wearing a sticker, badge, or gilt fish, as they become more and more well-known among non-Christians as our sign. It's also imperative to become a good car driver before sticking 'Thank God for Jesus' or the like on the back window, otherwise drivers following us will be doing anything but thanking God for Jesus.

But even without signs, stickers, or any other evangelism aid, Jesus is most powerfully proclaimed in living personal relationships. The sort where we're willing to put ourselves out for other people in need—for instance, to take children out to the park in the school holidays for a neighbouring harassed mum when we'd much rather stay in and read a good book. Or being willing to be a listening ear for a teenager in trouble who sometimes needs to talk and talk into the early hours. Or committing ourselves to visiting a lonely, elderly shut-in neighbour, and doing their shopping. Or being willing to go out to the pub, after an upbringing of never going near one, in order to be with neighbours on their own ground. And most of all, we need a relationship where we're willing to keep on being committed to whoever he sends, as a caring friend, until the friend becomes a sister or brother—or the Lord allows the commitment to change, through paths parting in one unavoidable way or another.

I thought that was about to happen recently with our postman. Though he only appears to be about forty, he's nearer sixty, and had decided he needed a less strenuous letter round than our very hilly route. So he swopped with a younger postman for a week's trial. As I thought back to our first conversation years before, I prayed silently about it. 'Lord, if you're still leading him to yourself through the Christians around here, please have him unhappy with that flatter route down the road, and somehow hankering for these hills again—even if it is at the price of a slower pace.'

The first time we'd exchanged more than 'hello' and 'thank-you' was one sparkling snowy day when the children were sledging on the field opposite our house. The postman arrived with his heavy sack overflowing with Christmas cards in the middle of a fresh snowstorm, so I offered him a cup of the coffee we'd just made, resisting pouring it into Stephanie's best Postman Pat mug—especially as our postman and Pat did rather resemble each other! And a minute later as his numb hands began to warm up and the coffee went down, Lucy and her friend Heather burst into the hallway. 'We're coming in to watch the telly for a bit and dry our gloves,' they said, 'and then we're sledging again, if that's all right.'

'I could do with you pulling my letters round on your sledge instead!' smiled Tom. 'It's nearly time I was off again.'

At the mention of time, Lucy looked down at her watch. 'Oh no,' she moaned, 'my new watch must have come loose and dropped off in the snow—and it could be in any of the fields across the road. We've been sledging in them all!'

'Well, I'm sorry,' replied this mean mother, 'but you'll just have to go straight back out and find it.'

'But it's impossible,' wailed Lucy. 'We've been sledging all over the fields, and the snow's ever so deep. We'll never find it in a million years.'

'If you ask Jesus to help you, though, you might,' I suggested. 'You try hard to retrace your steps, and we'll pray for God to guide you. Or rather we'll all pray right now, before you go, for God to show you where that watch is.' And, without more ado, I just prayed out loud, with a surprised postman at the side of me, 'Please Lord, can you shine your searchlight on that watch.' Which was just about what happened a minute or two later, but in a very unexpected way.

Lucy and Heather trudged back to the snowy fields, with even the now bright sunshine failing to inspire their seemingly impossible search. But it didn't really matter, because just as Tom was draining his coffee cup, there was a knock at the door, and there stood Pat, our nursery teacher friend who lived at the other side of the fields. She was arriving a bit early for our Thursday morning Bible study, and in her hands she held something really interesting. Staggeringly interesting in fact, because Pat was holding up Lucy's little watch, still ticking away, before our amazed eyes.

'I wonder whose . . .' began Pat, wondering why I was laughing.

'You'll never believe this,' I interrupted her, 'but just two minutes ago we prayed about a lost watch with Lucy and her friend.' (I hoped Tom didn't mind my including him in that polite 'we'!) 'You must have just missed seeing them—they probably began their search in the bottom field as you walked across to our house.'

'I can hardly believe it,' breathed Pat. 'Do you know, as I walked across the middle of the field opposite here I suddenly saw a little jewel glinting in the sun. So I went over to it and picked it up off the snow—and, lo and behold, it wasn't a jewel at all, but a buried watch with its winder uppermost, the only bit that showed.'

Even Tom looked amazed at such an instant answer to prayer—or, more probably for him, such an amazing coincidence. And when Lucy and Heather pushed disconsolately through the front-door half an hour later, saying, 'It's impossible,' they were thrilled to see it wasn't. Even though they'd missed their television programme they went back out to sledge with fresh enthusiasm, as well as warm gloves!

By then our postman friend had strode off into the snow again, but I knew without him saying that he wouldn't forget such an astonishing find, synchronised so perfectly with the spontaneous prayer he'd heard. And now he is happy to pray for people too, when I mention to him anyone particularly in need among the houses he visits, as I pass him on his rounds—now permanently committed to our hills. The Lord must have renewed his youth like the eagle's—or like the carrier pigeon's!

It's really fulfilling to see God bringing more and more people into his back-up teams, able to be the right person at the right time to deliver the goods, in prayer or in action. And just as God guided Pat's feet to exactly the right spot for her to see God's solar searchlight reflecting so brilliantly on the answer to our prayers, we too can be guided specifically in this exciting teamwork. The results don't depend on the importance of the need, but on the degree of dependency and expectation in our hearts.

That's the way it was the other day when I was circling round and round our town hall, trying to find a young lady in what could literally have been a life-and-death situation. Tracey was from London and had fled a violent boyfriend on discovering she was nearly two months pregnant. Having recently become a Christian, she'd come up north to Christian contacts but had been unable to find accommodation—except temporarily with overcrowded but kind Christian friends. Neither had she been able to find a job to pay off her debts, and with day-long debilitating sickness, she was beginning to despair. Abortion seemed the only practical way out. When she telephoned during the Tuesday fellowship meeting to say could I possibly pick her up as the council had been absolutely unable to help her, and her friend

had suggested the meeting might make a difference
somehow, I said I'd be right down. But when I arrived I
couldn't see Tracey among the crowds of shoppers, in
the area I thought she'd said she'd be. So I tried to circle
the widespread town hall buildings, with the exercise
made more difficult by one-way traffic signs here and
there—but still no sign of Tracey.

Knowing the Tuesday meeting might be her last
opportunity to hear God's answers to all her difficulties,
before abortion became cemented in her mind as the
only solution, I was praying desperately for help. Then
suddenly I saw Ken. He's a friend from a local house
church with a very caring heart. I stopped the car and
jumped out just in time to ask him, 'Ken, can you pray
that I'll find a young lady called Tracey, who's in great
need and should be somewhere around the town hall?'

Within five seconds of leaving Ken, I saw a tiny figure
waving at me from the furthest bend of the town hall.
Although I couldn't tell it was Tracey from that distance, she could obviously tell it was me. As we drove
back home, and Tracey shared all the details of her
situation, everything seemed hopeless. Her parents
were up in Cumbria, well-to-do but seemingly unable to
understand; the baby's father was impossibly violent;
and Sheffield was unable to supply the accommodation,
or, till then, the job she so desperately needed. But by
the time I drove Tracey to a house-church friend of
ours a few hours later, God had solved all her problems!
It began when the meeting split up into threes to pray
for each other and for whoever was on our hearts.

Tracey was in a triplet with Sally who was leading the
meeting, and Tracey's friend Sue. Sally didn't know
Tracey at all, but she received a word of knowledge

from the Lord about Tracey's parents being the solution to the predicament. Tracey would have tried to ignore such seemingly impossible advice, as her parents had already registered shock with accompanying non-involvement, on hearing their daughter's news. But somehow Sally communicated to Tracey that our only problem, ever, is finding out what God wants. And that when we do we are totally blessed in going his way, however hard his plan might seem. Then all of a sudden Tracey saw the light. She knew in her heart that the Lord needed her to phone her alienated parents. And she had that seemingly hard word confirmed when, on arriving home with Sue all ready to contact her parents, the phone rang—and it was her mum! She was full of compassion on hearing Tracey's news. Suddenly Tracey's parents really wanted her home!

It turned out they'd been attending a church where their faith had grown, and they'd been helping lots of young people. But now they wanted more than anything to help their own daughter. Not by being possessive, but by helping Tracey to find a flat and everything else she needed up there in Cumbria. Then, to add an extra 'hallelujah' to Tracey saying 'yes' to whatever God wanted, he provided a new friend, Lucy, from our local house church, who'd been through the same difficulties as Tracey some years before. She prayed in power for Tracey's more-than-morning sickness to disappear. And that's just what happened!

It's no wonder that God's team support beats the best that the world can supply in solving our problems, when he's able to impart out-of-this-world blessings through his mobile Holy Spirit containers. And his follow-up system can't be beaten, with the way he has total knowledge of every situation—and every person concerned—stored in his heavenly computers. Those heavenly computers, though, will probably turn out to be just part of an all-encompassing heart of love in the end. The love that he pours into the heart of every team member ready to move in compassion for him—with a back-up system that won't ever let us down.

15

Of Mice and Women!

Being a community carer can be very hard work, but when the Lord is in charge of the work and it is done to his instructions, even the laziest of saints can get excited about it—and grow addicted to it, too! When I was a teenager, being busy doing the Lord's work definitely meant a diary of prayer meetings, open-air work, Bible studies, and visiting the sick and elderly. Now, of course, the Lord's work can include such 'unspiritual' activities as going to the local keep-fit class—and not only to keep your personal high-tech physique in a first-class condition. You're also there to let him reach people who might otherwise never hear the good news.

The Lord's work for us, as people who care about our community, can include for instance visiting the local pub. And we don't go to distribute tracts to all the customers (though we would, of course, if the Lord showed us to one night). We go to meet people on their home ground, like Jesus did, so we can be available for anyone needing to relate to him as a person in that secular neighbourhood fellowship. Part of the church would still see such informal outreach as compromising with the enemy, and as condoning the drinking of alcohol. But sticking to fruit juice and entering into caring conversations no more condones alcohol than visiting patients in the local hospital condones illness.

And that's another way caring about the community works out in practice for some of us—taking Sunday morning 'gospel shows' into our local children's hospital (which are probably even more encouraging to the weary, worried parents staying with suffering offspring, than they are to the children themselves). The list of ways our Tuesday fellowship group (drawn from many denominations and many different backgrounds, from impoverished to very middle class) is useful in the community is as long as your arm. And 'the arms of love that compass me, would all mankind embrace'—that old Wesley hymn—sums up the motivation for people stretching themselves in service to others. Service as varied as setting up a neighbourhood baby-sitting circle, doing meals on wheels, taking school Christian assemblies, campaigning for a crossing at a very busy road junction, being on school boards of governors and running church playgroups. The service is sometimes specifically spiritual too, as lots of prayer group people demonstrated in distributing thousands of free monthly Christian newspapers—just as professionally produced, here in Sheffield, as the secular sort—through thousands of local doors. (For a Christian 'newspaper round', acquire either *The New Life* newspaper from TNL, 22 Copper Street, Sheffield, S3 7AG at 20p, or *Challenge* newspaper from CLF, Revenue Buildings, Chapel Road, Worthing, West Sussex, BN11 1BQ, at 16p a copy.)

One of the most exciting community action projects

our fellowship has fostered in prayer has been Cheriene's weekly aerobic class for her city church catchment
area. The prayer meeting that precedes each aerobics
session has been the key to that class answering the
needs of many young mums, particularly those feeling
shut in and unable to cope with demanding young
children. The crèche there is superbly run alongside the
class, and so many people (mainly young mums) have
been drawn in that three sessions are now needed for
the neighbourhood each week instead of one. Our
fellowship group is partly in existence for prayer
support for such brilliant evangelistic ventures, aimed in
the end at supplying needs of body, soul and spirit. And
regularly there are reports of people meeting Jesus
through outreach like the aerobics class and the Open
House coffee bar, and experiencing him working
miracles in all sorts of ways.

But basically the caring in the neighbourhood is
centred in pre-evangelism, producing a service that will
do people good whether or not they happen to meet
Jesus through it. And a service that always includes
personal caring for individuals just where they are and
as they are. Of course, it's more difficult for that
personal care to be demonstrated in more formal
situations, like in the comprehensive school Christian
assembly we support across the road from our house.
Being involved in that ministry to hundreds of teenagers each week keeps me communicating in up-to-the-
minute ways—and with previously unheard of words!
But even there the young people know they can arrange
to see one of the leaders after school about any need
they want to share, even though time doesn't allow for
personal contact at the end of the assembly.

Always, though, the most fruitful outreach into the community comes from consistency. Consistency produced by faithfulness, when the going with any sort of caring commitment gets tough. The sort of commitment shown by a Catholic neighbour, Mary, when many years ago she led a campaign to acquire a circular bus route through our very hilly neighbourhood where elderly people often found themselves stranded. With that community service battle successfully completed by two circular bus routes running hourly, Mary had the vision to begin a thriving Neighbourhood Network through holding a wildly successful royal wedding street party in her cul-de-sac. The 'Carter-Knowle Network' provided ventures as varied as school holiday seaside coach-trips and family lunches and enormously enterprising summer fairs, often drawing in many otherwise lonely, under-occupied people to discover the fun of working and playing hard together. Recently Mary's full-time management training job came to an end, and she said, 'What next, Lord?' He quickly showed her, when an elderly lady named Jean living a few doors up the road was suddenly bereaved of a sister. That sister had become Jean's indispensable right-hand woman since drastically poor circulation had caused her to lose a leg. Her shut-in life has been totally liberated through Mary's supervision of the house being beautifully and brilliantly transformed for easy management by a disabled person. And Mary's availability with others, in loving care for Jean's needs (and her Yorkshire terrier's needs too!), has provided her with all sorts of outside involvements as well. Especially since a ramp has been fitted to her front-door for an electric wheelchair. Now Jean has become involved in the community again too.

Another Tuesday fellowship member who is dynamic for her street in all sorts of ways is Lou, a young mum who was a nurse before beginning to work part time in her husband's printing business, since the arrival of little David. Children coming on the scene is often the signal for mums to become so taken up with home commitments that they have no time for outside involvements. But our Tuesday fellowship meeting runs an effective crèche, and anyway Lou is far too lively to let motherhood tie her to the house. Or to deprive David of the priceless training for life of seeing a mum living a life of service that makes sense—for him and his dad, as well as the community. In addition, I believe that knowing lots of unofficial aunties and uncles from an early age builds up confidence and outgoingness in toddlers no end. The most memorable time for me, however, of seeing Lou used by the Lord to benefit someone in the community happened when David was safely tucked up in bed.

Lou had come with me to take an evening service in a neighbouring Anglican church while the minister was away. I didn't realise, but that evening Lou was feeling awful, physically and spiritually. It's true that the enemy of our souls will always hit us while we're down, if he can, and he was certainly sustaining an attack on all fronts for Lou that night. But she was remembering hard the three short marching instructions for Christians contained in 1 Thessalonians 5:16–18. Those orders for God's freedom fighters in the thick of the battle are: 'Be joyful always, pray at all times, be thankful in all circumstances.' So even though Lou was feeling awful, she didn't tell me about it—she told the Lord instead, while she did her best to battle through for him.

The church we visited that night is a beautiful round building set on a hill, the wide, regularly spaced windows giving panoramic views of all over Sheffield. Seeing so many homes at once, representing so many needs, moved me to realise afresh that in the end only an all-knowing, all-powerful Lord who loves us totally, and takes everything and everybody into account, can satisfy everybody's needs at once. And knowing that seated in front of me was represented a microcosm of those needs I felt it right, as the service proceeded, to invite anyone with special problems to kneel at the altar rail for liberating prayer in Jesus' name. Since a stream of people came to the front as soon as I gave the invitation, I was very glad there were others there like Lou who were used to praying for people as the Holy Spirit directed.

I was aware a minute later though that Lou was still in her seat at the back of the church, because suddenly I needed her, knowing she must be the right person to pray for the lady who was telling me about her ill-health. Her main need was in suffering from a rare medical condition I'd never heard of—but I felt sure my nurse friend Lou would have. But just as I was about to look up to beckon Lou forward I had a reassuring surprise. There was Lou just moving down the aisle directly towards my distressed lady. I could never have guessed, as Lou had been such a brilliant actress for the Lord that evening, that she was coming forward in desperation, for prayer for herself! 'Lou, you have to be the right person to pray for my friend Mary, here,' I said. 'You really are hearing the Lord very loud and clear, because I was just that second going to beckon to you to come forward for Mary.' Lou smiled at me and immediately knelt beside her new sister to listen and minister, without my beginning to guess how she felt inside.

A few minutes later both Mary and Lou rose from their knees very much new women. Ministering rather than being ministered to was the last thing Lou had in mind when she'd sadly made her way to the front of the church that night. But in being used as a mighty channel of God's power for Mary, God had released Lou from her problems too, and without being prayed for at all she was able to go home rejoicing. She'd proved for herself that being temporarily unable to cope herself allowed God even more scope to cope for her, and to fill her with a fresh supply of the joy of the Lord. God's therapy for us when we're feeling hopeless is just the opposite to that of the world. The world says, 'Tell all your worries to everyone who will listen, to try and get them out of your system.' The trouble is that the more you talk about them, the worse they often appear—and you can grow addicted to their repetition, too! If they do temporarily diminish it's often only to return with renewed force when the kind listener is no longer there, and you realise that expressing your fears, doubts and miseries can often reinforce them.

A trouble shared, of course, can be gloriously a trouble halved when the problem is cared about and prayed about, and we're willing to let it go. Or when there's an easy practical answer we've been missing over a minor problem. Like what happened with Chris, the godsend-friend who came along when I was stuck over how to catch a mouse that had somehow invaded our kitchen. I couldn't bear to use a mouse trap, or poison. So Chris told me about slanting a milk bottle on the floor with a piece of chocolate dropped at the bottom, and at too steep an angle for a mouse to climb out again once its sweet tooth has been satisfied. (During a sojourn in a mouse-infested flat in inner London some years ago, Chris discovered very quickly that most mice prefer chocolate to cheese!) Then the next morning the intrepid milk bottle mouse can be freed in a neighbouring field or the like. That's a simple, if silly-sounding, example of how all sorts of practical problems can be solved when shared with the right friends.

(The same Chris is so spiritually strong and close to Jesus that God used her praying and weeping in the Spirit for an hour one night to wonderfully liberate a friend addicted to alcohol for many years, and this friend lived on the other side of the city to where Chris was exercised in prayer!)

But troubles that we keep to ourselves can make us miserable and tempt us to stay so, outwardly as well as inwardly. The only danger is rehearsing our troubles repeatedly, out of self-pity. 'Go ahead,' modern psychology says, 'express yourself. Better out than in.' But there's plenty more depression and misery where that came from; an unending supply in fact. And expressing it often just reinforces the misery habit pattern. (I'm not describing the situation where someone needs psychiatric help, or needs prayer and inner healing, or deliverance, for something which has not been shared productively before. Even in those situations, though, the sufferer has to stop reciting their troubles when all the necessary information has been shared—as one friend of mine couldn't do. Then, one glorious day, after relating all her troubles to her psychiatrist for the umpteenth time, he interrupted with, 'You are never going to get better!' and left. After being in agony for an hour, she realised that winning the battle was up to her—and has been a winner ever since!)

The Lord's way is different from the world's. He uses inner healing and deliverance to set us free. Then he says, 'If any man will come after me, let him deny himself, and take up his cross, and follow me' (Matthew 16:24, AV). And with Lou's Thessalonians instructions too, he's reminding us that his psychology often works the other way round to the sort we're used to. When we tell the Lord our troubles instead of involving other people, and then act as if everything is fine (because God says it in his word, whatever we're thinking or feeling), it very soon is!

And it very soon was for Lou, that night, as she walked forward for her own needs and found God's deliverance came in seeing to someone else's.

Another way God uses Lou, along with an increasing number of others in our weekly fellowship meeting, is in fasting as well as praying, when the Lord directs for special needs. Sometimes people join in sponsored fasts to aid the Third World. But more often people undertake spontaneous fasts under God's direction for needs in the meeting and in the community, having checked their fitness medically. Not that fasting can possibly force God's arm to do what we want, or anything like that, but we've found that in fasting we're much better enabled to hear God's voice, and to know the prayers he wants us to pray for those in need. We can see more clearly how to pray against Satan's strategies too.

Many of us also eat more sensibly for our health and strength's sake when we discover the physical benefits of fasting, especially potentially greedy people like me!

And we spend more sensibly too, as we enjoy a simpler diet. (Our Tuesday fellowship meeting has sent more than £2,000 over the years to people in every sort of need, at home and abroad, through a roomful of us sharing a bread-and-water lunch once a month, and giving and praying accordingly.) When God shows us to fast for prayer-power reasons, an increasing number of us are ready. And some of us are ready for anything, from a total, days-long water fast, to a fruit juice fast, to a partial fruit and vegetable fast, to even just missing one meal, for beginners. Somehow the discipline of cutting out food sharpens our spiritual awareness, and then we know how to pray in power.

And that's the way Cheriene and I travelled one day to take a meeting that unbeknown to us was going to touch a whole community—missing our breakfasts, I mean! We were going to speak to a ladies' coffee morning organised in a nearby Derbyshire market town. And we prayed conversationally with the Lord as I drove the car over to Matlock for the meeting, for all the people he wanted to reach there. (Particularly the people who didn't yet even know about the meeting, but whom God was needing to nudge to go along, maybe through a neighbour dropping in on their way there. That prayer has often been seen to be powerfully answered.) As we drove along I suddenly realised I'd left the directions on the mantlepiece back home as I'd loaded the car. So that little surprise added fresh fuel to our prayers. And in the amazing way God does these things, on arriving in Matlock, we kept on 'sensing' where to turn, and when. We didn't ask for directions until we happened to be on the very street where the church hall was situated, and almost opposite it. I guess that was a good example of the way fasting sharpens the ability to sense God's leading, practically as well as spiritually. It wasn't long before Cheriene was sharing how she'd met Jesus, with a packed room. She is the very successful head of a dancing school, and was the youngest-ever dancing examiner to travel the country—until she realised that job ambition was coming destructively first in her life, and hurting her young family too. From that realisation she began to search for what should come first, and found, not it, but him.

Her testimony, and my talk, led to a number of people requesting prayer at the end of the meeting (including an old school friend I'd not seen for twenty years, who had moved to Derbyshire to run a cafe and gem-stone business with her husband). Right at the end of the queue was an elderly farmer's wife who was obviously very strained by exertion. As she sat in the 'prayer chair' she told Cheriene and myself how her heart was in an appalling state, and that the doctor had warned her to stay at home indefinitely. I wasn't surprised, seeing her cyanosed condition, and inwardly prayed, 'Lord, make our faith firm enough for Mabel.' Then I began to pray out loud.

Cheriene hadn't been a believer for very long, so usually I tended to pray out loud while she prayed silently both in English and in the heavenly language God had given her. After we'd asked Mabel about herself and her illness, I prayed first for her to feel the Lord's anointing as we laid hands on her shoulders together. 'And please, Lord, wash us all afresh in your precious blood and fill us with your Holy Spirit's power—and help Cheriene and myself to hear your voice,' I added with feeling, knowing Mabel was needing very powerful prayer to survive such a bad heart condition. Then I prayed about everything I could think of. I prayed for her heart, for her circulation, and for healing to flow, in Jesus' name. When she still seemed no different I prayed that Satan and his agents would be prevented from oppressing her; for her relationships with the Lord and other people to be right; for 'by his stripes we are healed' (Isaiah 53:5) to apply; for her to be truly born again if she wasn't quite already; for her to receive inner healing for her emotions if they needed it; for her to be able to forgive anyone she might have anything against—and then I ran out of prayers to pray!

'Er, Mabel, can you think of any other possible blockage to your healing?' I enquired. 'Eeh, don't worry, dear,' she confided in her soft Derbyshire accent. 'I was healed the minute you started to pray for me! I knew I would be.'

I stared at her, incredulously. 'You see,' she continued, 'when I woke up this morning I was so ill I couldn't even move. I'd really wanted to come to this meeting—it's not often something like this happens here. And I'd invited a non-Christian friend from the village to come with me. So I cried out, "Lord, the doctor's told me I'm not to move, and he can't do anything to improve my heart but, Doctor Jesus, you can give me a new heart, let alone heal this one. So please will you heal me enough to get to the meeting, for my friend's sake?" And as soon as I asked him,' Mabel added 'I felt new power surging into me. Enough to get out of bed, and then enough to get dressed, and then to get here with my friend. And somehow I knew he was going to finish off healing my heart once I'd arrived here. And so he has,' she smiled at us, with total confidence.

Cheriene looked as if she too had been aware of God's healing in a wonderful way all the time, and as often happens I thanked God for the sister he'd sent to pray with me, aware of how much more God's power can flow where two or three of us are united together. And of how the sisters he gives me are often so much more God's 'unblocked drainpipes' for his blessings to flow through than I am. But for any of us, if we've only faith the size of a grain of mustard seed, we've enough faith to pray—however haltingly.

However, faith to know exactly what God has done is different. My faith was still tinged with the logical knowledge that Mabel could still need more healing for that badly damaged heart of hers, although I didn't say so because God hadn't made it clear to me.

A year later, though, he did. I was attending a weekend celebration at Derbyshire's Cliff College Methodist training centre. The college is surrounded by beautiful grounds in the middle of the glorious Derbyshire Dales, with adjacent fields used as car-parks for the vast number of Whitsuntide visitors. As I was climbing up the slope from our aged Datsun to the college, with the children in tow, I heard someone shouting, 'Hilary!' Running up the hill behind us was someone I vaguely remembered. Was she a dental patient, a radio interviewee, or a lady from one of the many churches I visit in the course of the year?

A moment later I discovered that she was from none of those groups at all. She was one of the ladies at the coffee morning in Matlock those many months ago. 'I'm so glad I've seen you,' she said. 'I'm Mabel's friend, and as well as that meeting being a great blessing to me, Mabel's been a new woman ever since. Her heart is totally healed since you and your friend prayed, and it's been a wonderful witness to all the village, who knew she'd no hope of getting better. Isn't Jesus wonderful!'

Well, I guess I'll never get over how wonderful he is, and how every day afresh there's more of his wonder to discover. But what thrills me most of all is when, like with Mabel, he blesses one person and the whole community is able to see without a shadow of doubt that Jesus is alive. And that he cares about any of us who cry to him for help. He's the very best community carer there could ever be! But he's committed himself to needing neighbours to accomplish his love revolution, right where we live. So let's open our hearts to need any neighbours he sends—for his sake, for their sake, and definitely for ours!

WORK-OUT 5
Neighbours in the Community

'Good fences make good neighbours.'
(*Robert Frost, 1873–1963*)

'Nor knowest thou what argument
  Thy life to thy neighbours' creed has lent
All are needed by each one . . .'
(*Ralph Waldo Emerson 1803–82*)

1. GIVE AND TAKE
'I could be really good if it weren't for other people!'
This comment, voiced by our frustrated twelve-year-old
after trouble from a playground fight, sums up humanity's main problem—personally, nationally and inter-
nationally. Caring co-operation is the only answer to
relationship problems, particularly if co-operation with
Christ and surrender to him is the starting point.
  Read Matthew 5:1–16.

(a) In what ways can our lives be salt and light in our
    neighbourhoods before our words are heard?
(b) Should Christians allow themselves to be put upon
    in expressing Christ's agape love?
(c) 'Satan finds work for idle hands to do.' In what ways
    can we best help unemployed young people, who
    hang about the streets with time on their hands (a)
    to come into a relationship with Jesus Christ; (b) to
    keep occupied until employment materialises?
(d) Should every Christian's home be an 'open home' to
    some extent? What about partners who aren't

202

Christians? How can *your* home be more open for the Lord?

2. TEAM SUPPORT
Read Acts 13:4–12.

(a) Have you any experience of signs and wonders helping non-believers come to faith? (It's interesting, when time allows, individually to read through the Acts of the Apostles noting how often it states that the church grew after miracles of healing and other signs and wonders, particularly 'raising the dead'.)

(b) In combating forces of evil we need to be firmly under God's protection. How can we ensure this?

(c) If 'faith without works is dead' (James 2:17), what 'works' are needed to help people in our own individual neighbourhoods, for faith to spread? How many non-Christian friends do we have, and where can we go to make more? And how can our fellowships best help unmarried mums when we've encouraged them to keep their babies?

(d) Might some Christians need to build 'good fences' where they are at the beck and call of neighbours' indiscriminate needs? How can they do this?

3. OF MICE AND WOMEN!
Read 2 Timothy 3:10–4:5.

(a) How much should we be 'instant in season [and] out of season' (AV) in gossiping the gospel? Will such seemingly indiscriminate evangelism alienate more people than it attracts?

(b) How best can we help people who've become addicted to attention seeking, and too comfortable in their afflictions to want to change?

(c) What sort of faith is 'faith as a grain of mustard seed'? What other sorts of faith are there?

(d) How can each of us be increasingly empowered to 'love our neighbours as ourselves'? Have we ever asked God to find us a Christian neighbour, willing to pray with us each week for our neighbourhood?

Praise Point: '. . . that you, being rooted and established in love . . . may be filled to the measure of all the fulness of God' (Ephesians 3:18–19, NIV).

EPILOGUE

Beyond the Limit

One of the very best ways to practise loving our neighbours, whoever they are, is to find someone else who wants to do likewise—and to hear God's instructions together. Once we're committed to praying regularly with one or two others for the neighbours around us, we find ourselves beginning to like all sorts of unlikely people—and then to love them too. God's psychology works the other way round from the world's. He tells us to act as if we love people even though we don't, and then we'll gradually—and sometimes immediately—feel we do. The world says, 'Wait till your feelings are right and you have your act sorted out before you start.' But God says to start straight away, ignoring our feelings, and as we obey the command to act out his love for people, we'll find he gives us all the good feelings we'll ever need. We have limits on who we can love, but God takes us beyond the limit to discover his joy with people we once couldn't stand. He has us sit down with them instead because sometimes the first people we learn to appreciate like that are the very people God has given us to pray with!

That was the way it was for me when we first moved to the 'Cookhouse'. The name is totally appropriate in both senses, with the countless number of people who consume 'Cookhouse fare' each week. Even young Lucy can bake a tray of buns ready to eat in twenty minutes from start to finish, for unexpected visitors. The 'Cookhouse' speciality isn't home-baking though. It's Living Bread. But I spent my first few months here keeping to myself this hungry world's best-kept secret—that Jesus is alive and brings overflowing life to everyone who asks—though I desperately wanted to share it.

I knew that evangelism is just one beggar telling another beggar where to find bread. But I also knew that caring, sharing prayer is essential to the good news being communicated in relevant ways, in words and deeds. It's no good trying to force unwanted good news on people who aren't yet interested. So with 'whenever two of you on earth agree . . .' (Matthew 18:19) ringing in my ears, I set about trying to find someone else similarly motivated. But it was to no avail until the Lord answered my heart's desire for a prayer partner by creating a brand-new believer. You can read about my astonishing sister Val in *What will the neighbours say?*, but missing from that book is how we, though neighbours, are poles apart. Even our besetting sins were totally different!

And every prayer partner the Lord has provided since has involved a temperament clash, as if to keep us relying on Jesus instead of on each other. For instance, one friend had been the talk of the district for her vitriolic bad temper before she met Jesus, but I usually indulged in the opposite anger response of retreating into silent self-pity and resentment when things didn't go my way. She was basically a solitude loving saint (though a gifted communicator and teacher), and I was a gregarious person with an embarrassingly simple down-to-earth faith. And if God hadn't given us the task of praying together, I guess we would soon have become irritated by each other's personalities, and decided that 'love your neighbour' applied to somebody else.

It's amazing, though, how practice makes perfect, even in concentrating on other people's good points instead of their bad ones. And in putting ourselves in other people's places too. There's probably not a soul on this planet without some quality either to admire or empathise with, if we're willing to look hard enough— and willing to ask for the Lord's love for that person, too. One of my goal verses from the Bible is Paul's amazing statement, 'I have learned, in whatsoever state I am, therewith to be content' (Philippians 4:11, AV). And that from a man who was persecuted and imprisoned many times!

The lesson in that verse reminds me of Richard, who, you'll remember, gave the rest of his already long life to the Lord when he was staying in one of the bedsits up the road. Richard had plenty of turn-offs about him, like a sickening smell (which we gradually eliminated with a few homely hints, and a set of 'new' clothes) and two-inch fingernails, where they weren't demolished to nicotine-stained stubs. I'd have offered to cut them if I could have steeled myself, but instead I let them get in the way of my being able to appreciate Richard at all. And even when our kind next-door neighbour, Keith, cut them for him I still had trouble accepting him. But all that animosity changed on the day of the move.

We were moving Richard into a pokey little bedsit

he'd chosen because a friend already lived in the same house, close to the main road. His new room was so narrow and dingy that it looked worse than a prison cell. And it was in the attic of a house that smelled almost as bad as he had done! On top of that, his hopeless heart and lungs made the steep, dark stairs seem like Mount Everest. And the time-switch light went out even before he'd arrived, panting, at the first landing. I was horrified at the thought of *anyone* moving into such a hovel.

But, as we finished carting Richard's meagre possessions up the stairs and setting them out, he stood back really satisfied and waved an arm expansively around his tiny, shabby domain. 'Well, how do you like it?' he beamed, looking really proud of his new territory. I could see in his face that happy 'no place like home' look. He was as pleased as if he'd just moved into Buckingham Palace. *Forgive me, Lord*, I thought, ashamed of all my dissatisfaction with our comparative palace, and of the way I took it for granted. Now I knew I really could love Richard just as he was, filled with admiration for this 'moving' virtue of his great thankfulness for small mercies, and the contentment that goes with it.

God gives us plenty of practice at loving whomever he sends, living where we do. That's because our next-door neighbours, Keith and Maureen, bought their house especially to share with people in need of care (and sometimes loving discipline) in order to get them straightened out—as well as to be 'home' to anyone else the Lord sends, with or without problems. The bedsit tenants almost always turn out to be as much blessings as blessed, God's 'love your neighbour' instructions including lots of sacrificial give and take. And even though we might often start by doing almost all the giving, as Keith and Maureen have done so often, sticking with a relationship that God has brought about always leads to receiving on both sides. Even if only in learning valuable spiritual lessons. But the giving often works out in other ways too.

One of next door's tenants who needed a lot of prayer and practical friendship was Christina, a retired university geologist. She was Dutch, but had married an English geology professor many years before. A series of sad family circumstances led one night to her falling down on her knees by her bed and calling out, 'Jesus, if you're there, please take over my life.' And immediately Christina knew God's love was enveloping her like a warm blanket, and she heard the Lord's voice telling her just how much he loved her. With that transforming start to her new life with Jesus, it wasn't surprising that she found she could often hear the Lord speaking to her—for other people as well as for herself. Although she had many problems still to work out when her husband left her to live in Spain and she came to stay next door, the time spent helping her was often give-and-take time. Even Christina's smile was an encouraging gift for anyone attempting to help this highly intelligent but deeply hurt woman. And her flashes of insight for other people seemed to operate even when her own problems were occupying far too much of her—and everyone else's—time.

Tales of her childhood in the Dutch East Indies provided amusing entertainment for our children when Christina was having a good day. And her Indonesian spicy lamb recipe was an instant favourite with our family from the day she came round to cook it for us. As were the Peking pork delights, with accompanying Chinese delicacies, that Christina's attic-room successor, Xioubai, painstakingly prepared for us. He was a Chinese communist computer research student from the university. His room and his lifestyle were very spartan, but he revelled in family life and had a tremendous love for children. And the beginnings of a love for the Lord, even, before he left for his faraway home and family.

We also quite often find ourselves enjoying Pakistani and Kashmiri food as we befriend more and more Muslim families moving into our area and they send round dishes of their national delicacies for us (although sometimes 'enjoy' isn't quite the right word, depending on the strength of seasoning). So then it's very gratifying to pass on anything beyond our palates' appreciation to the rather poverty-stricken and ever-growing Muslim family living a few doors along from the bottom of our garden. As we can't tell them the sources of their periodic surprises, they're probably amazed at my seemingly extensive culinary skills. I just hope I'm never asked for the recipes!

Contacts with our Asian neighbours have meant more than one miraculous answer to prayer for them, with Jesus seen to be the source of the power involved. That was particularly so on the day one-year-old Camran wandered half a mile over busy roads to our main shopping centre, while his parents and six brothers and sisters searched frantically for him. Then two of the sisters, who've discovered the power of prayer in Jesus' name, thought to run round to our neighbour Joan to ask her to pray. And minutes later the family saw it as no coincidence that a police car containing the well-travelled toddler happened to pass their house—though the police had scores of streets and more to check for an anxious Pakistani family searching for their lost toddler. So we pray that one day as we keep sharing our lives—and sharing our food together too—we might even find ourselves sharing the Living Bread with one or two of our Asian friends.

Going back to Christina, she finally felt strong enough in her walk with Jesus to return to Spain where she and her ex-husband had made their home together for much of their lives. But most of all she was moving over there as an unofficial missionary for Jesus Christ, whatever way the Lord might be going to work out her family relationships. And we were all thrilled that Keith and Maureen's sacrifice in opening their home to whomever the Lord might send had again resulted in blessings all round. Now that Maureen has been suffering increasingly from Parkinson's disease for the last few years, the Lord keeps sending wonderful helpers to live in the house when a bedsit becomes vacant, without any arranging on Keith or Maureen's part.

Like Gail, who moved in due to her friend Dave, a committed Christian, being there, but who didn't herself have anything to do with his faith or with Christians in general. She'd scowl around at us when we talked about the Lord, and disappear as soon as she could. But within a month, because she didn't want to waste a meal-ticket for a gospel dinner when Maureen couldn't go, Gail had seen the light! And she came home from that dinner quite drunk in the Spirit, and filled with the joy of the Lord due to the prayers she'd happily received after going forward to commit her life to Jesus. What a transformation from the miserable, doing-her-duty agnostic I'd driven over to the dinner. The reason she had felt compelled to go reluctantly to the front of the meeting to ask Jesus to take over her life was the thought that, if the speaker was right about Jesus, that invitation might be her last chance to get her life sorted out. So she went forward in case, and found herself immediately aware that the speaker was right and that she'd discovered the reason for living.

And now the reason for her being next door is wonderfully obvious to Maureen, as Gail is her ever-present help in every way, while Maureen looks forward to the healing the Lord has for her, having already received his first instalment—for her face and feet! Neighbours have stayed up all night in prayer for Maureen, and many friends and neighbours have fasted and prayed for all God's best blessings for her, so we know there are more on the way.

Of course, there are stories of apparent failure to recount as well as success, in our house as well as next door; and in our lives as well as of those to whom we minister. The definition of a back-slidden Christian (as someone who was once closer to the Lord than they are at the moment) continually reminds us of our need to put Jesus first in our lives more and more. Obedience to him is the key to our hearing his voice in such clarity that his plans work out both for us and for anyone else in need. That obedience causes the love, joy and peace that are part of the fruit of the Spirit to blossom and flourish in our lives. And it causes the gifts of the Spirit, like discernment and wisdom for particular needs, and healing and deliverance, to be available whenever necessary too.

However, we can block God's day-by-day plan for our lives and the lives of others very easily, by insisting on our own way, and by neglecting to ask, 'What next, Lord?' as a matter of course whenever there are options. Now every day begins with me asking God to make me very sensitive to his voice, and to everyone else's. And I'm grateful for the people in my life who regularly hear the Lord's voice more clearly than I do, encouraging me to listen more, through the miracles that happen as they love their neighbours the Lord's way.

Being available to our neighbours means that David and I work doubly hard at making sure the children don't miss out. One way God has guided us for family togetherness is to enjoy a weekly banquet together. Every Tuesday we take it in turns to choose the menu for our special family meal, deciding on anything from toad-in-the-hole to chicken à la crème, with recurring requests for beefburgers and beans every time it's the younger end's turn! For three hours we keep the door locked and detach the phone. (Except when it's our turn to be on evening call for our local Message helpline telephone service. Instead, those nights, we ask the Lord to keep people from ringing till after our celebration, and he always does, unless there's a very special reason otherwise.) The meal over, we'll play games for an hour—anything from mixed triples tennis on the courts in the field across the road from us, to tiddley winks on the cleared table. And then the little ones will have a specially long story—sometimes the never-ending saga of James Jerollorum Jiggs, straight from the more fanciful regions of my mind. Altogether a very refreshing and strengthening family time for us all. And a time that has us all grow stronger to help the people the Lord sends.

One of those people was Katey. She was one of the

friends I'd been praying for with Maureen next door and in our small weekly neighbourhood prayer group. Katey was a sixth-former at the comprehensive school across the road, and her parents were members of our church. As part of her theology A-level studies she'd been asking me about the house groups meeting in our home. Sensing that Katey was basically an agnostic, I told her about our Thursday morning beginners' Bible study as well as the Tuesday morning fellowship meeting, hoping to communicate that the Bible is far more than a theology textbook—more like the Manufacturer's Handbook and the twentieth-century miracle-workers' compendium all rolled into one! I told her about the money we'd raised over the years through those monthly bread-and-water lunches (in aid of all sorts of people in need around the world) to communicate one of the ways that evangelical Christians care about the wider community. And I told her also about the miracles God works in our midst in bringing people from darkness to light, hoping she might want to meet this miracle-working God for herself. But Katey seemed totally unconvinced. So one Tuesday morning a week or two later I had a double surprise.

The first surprise was in seeing a handful of people arrive for the cancelled meeting—it was a half-term holiday and we'd decided the week before that there would be too many of us away to meet that Tuesday. But there were at least a dozen people who hadn't got the message and, to my amazement, Katey suddenly arrived at the door too. 'I thought I'd come and sample the meeting for myself,' she explained, slightly embarrassed. And I was more than slightly embarrassed as I started to lead the totally unplanned get-together with my mind empty of anything that would impress a questioning theology student!

Usually we take it in turns for a couple of people each week to lead the meeting and to prepare a short Bible study for it, but this morning it looked as if I'd be doing both, with no preparation whatsoever. I knew the Holy Spirit was the real leader of the meeting, so I shouldn't have worried. But I did, because I was too taken up with impressing my new neighbour, Katey, rather than loving her. As often happens, though, moving into singing God's praises lifted me into a longing for everyone to be able to enjoy the Lord's presence together. I forgot all about Katey needing to be impressed by us, or needing to see that our theology made sense—or even seeing her need of Jesus. She was just one of a group of people whose lives could be liberated in worship there and then. After that God nudged some of us into sharing Bible passages that had done us good. And then people mentioned prayer needs—their own and other people's. The meeting was flowing beautifully when suddenly the phone rang.

The caller's voice somehow seemed familiar. 'You might have forgotten me by now, but I'm Chris, and I came to your house each Tuesday a few years ago. I've recently had a baby, and both of us are rather poorly. I'm ringing halfway through the meeting because I've only just woken up from snatching an hour's sleep. I've been awake all night with the baby crying, and with pain from my post-natal complications. So I'm just wondering if I might walk over if you think the meeting will go on for a while yet?' Part of me thought, *Oh, Lord, you know I need it to be a short meeting because I promised to take the children out, and I haven't a car today, and it'll take Chris half an hour to walk here.* But then I remembered that the Lord knew best so I told Chris it would be lovely to see her, and whatever time she arrived there would be someone here available to pray for her and little Luke. As Chris was a believer who'd been unable to have fellowship with other Christians for a long time, just being with other believers would do her good, for a start.

People were heavily into praying for neighbourhood needs when I tiptoed back into the room. Glancing at Katey, I was relieved to see she wasn't gazing around looking bored. In fact she looked as if she was as intent on praying as everyone else; though I could have been fooled, as pretending to pray is the easiest pretence of all! Soon I was lost in prayer myself and forgot all about Chris until I heard the front-door opening just as someone started off a praise song. In walked a very wan-looking young woman, with a tiny baby in her arms, suddenly taking everyone's attention. By now we were well back into singing and praising again, so Chris settled down in the armchair someone had vacated for her. She looked as if she might suddenly be joining her soundly-sleeping son. Time was running out and it was only a little while before I was inviting everyone to share the grace together. Usually we link hands as we pray that short closing prayer, but today the procedure was interrupted by Beryl, our next-door neighbour, exclaiming, 'Katey, are you all right? Your hands feel incredibly hot.'

Everyone stared at the embarrassed sixth-former. But I stared even harder when I heard Katey's reply. 'Yes, I'm OK,' she stammered, 'but the only Christian book I've ever read said about your hands growing hot when

God wants to heal through you; and I think that must be happening to me. So I'm wondering,' Katey added hesitantly, 'whether anyone here needs healing.' At that, Chris (who hadn't said a word about her need, except to me on the phone) gave the baby to the delighted lady on her left and pulled herself to her feet. 'I'm sure it must be me because when I woke after a short sleep an hour or two ago, the Lord somehow made me aware that I should come here to be healed of my post-natal complications.'

Never having seen Katey before, Chris presumed she must be used to praying for healing for people. So she crossed the room and stood expectantly before her, eyes closed in prayer. Poor Katey knew she'd no choice, though she'd never spontaneously prayed out loud in her life before. All this time I was gazing incredulously at my young friend. I thought she'd come to the meeting to be an impartial observer, or worse! And here she was about to pray for healing for the person God had sent specifically to receive it. Or was she . . .?

Katey looked decidedly nervous, as well she might. But something wonderful indeed must have happened to her since her last visit, I realised. Because suddenly she *did* begin to pray. 'Please God, supply Chris' need, and heal her body so that . . .' But before Katey had finished her prayer, I became even more open-mouthed because Chris was suddenly horizontal instead of vertical—laid out in the middle of our front-room floor, eyes closed, and looking full of peace and joy. Which was just how Katey looked a moment later as she realised what God had done for her new sister. (As sometimes happens with prayer for healing, the power of the Holy Spirit was so strong that Chris' nerve-muscle conduction system was somehow taken over, as God's force for healing started to work. And the effect is rather like an anaesthetic being used by a surgeon—or dental surgeon—to render the patient unconscious while the surgery is performed. But God's surgery heals the soul as well as the body, hence the peace and joy the 'patient' feels. The state is easily faked by attention-seekers, of course, but that doesn't negate the authentic gift of God.)

As Chris lay there, eyes closed, she caused a minor crisis in the front garden. One of the taller children looked through the window and called out, 'Come quickly everyone—someone's mum's lying dead in the middle of the floor!' Suddenly a row of children's faces peered in impassively, while one of the little ones, who couldn't quite see, remembered his mum saying that morning that he'd be the death of her one day. His worry was short-lived though, as one of the others gave him a leg-up, and he glimpsed his mum safe and singing at the other side of the room. 'I didn't think I'd been that naughty, Mum,' he said afterwards!

Chris lay 'resting in the Spirit' all through the final celebratory song and well into the shared lunch, with children stepping carefully over her and trying not to drop crumbs on her too much as they helped themselves from the trolley! But my amazement was still centred on how God used the youngest new-born member of his family that morning—and maybe the newest Christian in the whole city—to heal Chris in such a spectacular way. (Katey told me later how reading *Nine O'Clock in the Morning* just after she'd seen me, had led her to ask Jesus to take over her life there and then, for whatever he wanted to do with it.)

Many times since then, Katey has been God's 'drainpipe' for healing, and sometimes for other gifts of the Spirit to flow through as well. It is a great discovery when we realise that God doesn't need us to have any qualifications to be used by him for passing on his miracle-working power. All he needs is for us to make sure we become empty 'drainpipes' with no blockages in our lives to hinder his gifts from flowing through us to a world full of desperately needy people—blockages like pride, self-interest, disobedience, greed, resentment or self-pity. And then we discover that any and every gift of the Spirit is able to be channelled through us, as the needs arise, and that the best gifts Paul tells us to desire earnestly in 1 Corinthians 12:31 are whichever gifts are going to be the most appropriate in each needy situation—whether healing, prophecy, tongues, dis- cernment, interpretation or whatever.

Often human talents are needed to operate with the spiritual dynamite too. And discovering and supplying people's needs has to be bathed in self-denying love. It's the love which the Bible tells us (1 Peter 4:8) covers a multitude of sins, maybe for the person exercising it as well as the one receiving it. It's the love that is willing to go the second mile, while refusing to start on even the shortest ego trip, and the love that enables God to inspire us to even more usefulness to him. And, again, it's the love that often has hardly anything to do with feelings, but everything to do with commitment. Commitment to God, leading us to commitment to the neighbour he needs us to help.

For some of us, that might mean being willing to commit ourselves overseas, coping with strange food, oppressive climates, insects everywhere and maybe cardboard shanty towns, intersected by open sewers, or no sewers at all! Or it might mean committing ourselves to the inner city here in the western world, with our windows broken every week, our children in over-populated, understaffed schools with minimum facilities, and our home regularly entertaining down-and-outs who tax our Christian love to the limits. Or it could mean committing ourselves to being 'tentmakers', taking our skills overseas to work maybe low profile in a Muslim environment, by being salt and light there. Or perhaps we might find ourselves in an English country village where things have remained the same for the last half century, and there's going to be resistance to a radical Christian lifestyle, with shared homes and signs and wonders shocking people's complacency over their distant impersonal God.

Sometimes too that commitment can lead us into new territory spiritually as well as physically, as I discovered when I asked God to show me how I could be of more use to him. Especially for helping neighbours in need, in heaven-sent ways. Suddenly everything I heard and read seemed to have something to do with that embarrassing gift of speaking in tongues. Embarrassing to me because I'd asked others for prayer a number of times for anointing to speak in tongues—but still I couldn't! However, I *could* make up sounds that came across like my friends speaking in tongues, and because I'd often seen situations dramatically change when Christians praised God in tongues, I was desperate enough to say, 'Father, I'm going to use this made-up tongue as if it were the real thing unless and until you show me I shouldn't, or change it into the reality.' So, like Jackie Pullinger in *Chasing the Dragon*, I set my alarm clock for twenty minutes earlier each morning to practise my 'home-made' speaking in tongues, hopefully for long enough to edify myself, or build myself up in the faith, as the Bible implies should happen (1 Corinthians 14:4). But my main reason for wanting to speak in tongues was to be able to worship God without running out of words—as happens to me far too quickly in English!

I didn't feel strengthened by the practice at first, but I kept reminding myself that we're not meant to take notice of our feelings as Christians, more of our facts as the Bible states them. So I'd continued with this seemingly sterile exercise for a whole month when I found myself travelling into Derbyshire to take a Sunday evening service at an old Methodist Church in New Mills. As the service neared its end I suddenly felt quite certain that God was wanting to heal someone there of a physical ailment. This sort of revelation was totally new to me, but I felt it strongly enough to know I had to tell the congregation.

'It must be me!' said a young woman with a strong Derbyshire accent, starting to walk forward at my invitation a moment later. This sort of carry-on was obviously new to most of the congregation, so I suddenly thought of how to include them in it. 'I wonder if there's anyone who might join me in praying for Jenny, here at the front? You don't have to verbalise your prayers, but just laying a hand in love on Jenny's shoulder as we all pray together could be part of God's power supply for our sister.' I was really grateful to see two middle-aged ladies walk out nervously to stand on either side of Jenny—particularly as my prayers for Jenny's healing wouldn't seem too way out to the congregation if their own members were involved.

As I heard from Jenny, a minute later, of her need for healing after a failed abdominal operation, my heart went out to her. The operation had caused adhesions, giving the mother of a small, lively child almost too much pain to cope with. A second operation had failed to put things right, so the next day Jenny was going into hospital for tests before a third operation would hopefully redress the damage. So I felt really motivated for the Lord to use us any way he could, to bring healing to poor Jenny and spare her yet another operation. And it was a good thing I did, because I soon realised that Jenny's two friends weren't going to pray out loud, and after I'd asked the Lord to work the miracle she needed, I suddenly knew he was saying something desperately embarrassing to me. 'What about praying in that heavenly language now?' I seemed to hear. I had to think hard of Jenny's suffering to force myself into co-operating with that heavenly voice, and perhaps shocking my very un-Pentecostal congregation. Just when I felt I'd worshipped our healing Lord long enough in my seemingly made-up heavenly language (knowing that the quiet, intercessory speaking in tongues was private prayer and praise for Jenny, and not for public interpretation), I realised something even worse!

This time that inner voice really took my breath away—but not quite enough, because the Holy Spirit's suggestion meant I was going to need my breath even more. He wanted me to sing in the Spirit, in front of everyone, for the sake of Jenny and the healing she needed so badly. I had sometimes varied my twenty minutes of speaking in tongues with a short burst of singing instead, so at least I was becoming *used* to singing in the Spirit—but not in front of a massed audience. I wanted to die, but immediately realised I might as well die to myself instead and get it over with. So I forced myself to obey the Lord again, and for half a minute embarrassed the congregation, Jenny and myself by flowing up and down the scales in my synthetic language. So it wasn't really a surprise at the end of such a way-out exhibition, to hear an uninhibited Jenny complain loudly for all to hear, 'Well, I don't know what you've done, but when you sang it felt as if you'd turned me insides the other way up!'

Oh no, Lord. Will I ever hear you right? I groaned inwardly. But I made comforting noises to Jenny, and polite farewells to everyone else shortly afterwards. And that was that. Or so I thought. But the next night I had the surprise of my life. It was a phone call from a friend of Jenny's to tell me about Jenny's amazing hospital visit.

She'd seen the consultant that afternoon, and he'd been quite cross with the nurse on examining Jenny and then her notes. 'These can't possibly be this patient's notes,' he informed the nurse. 'Go and find where they've got to!' And, just as the nurse was wondering what to do, another doctor passed the door and saw Jenny's coat with a Jesus badge on it. 'Oh, if you're having trouble with notes, don't worry,' he called through to his learned colleague. 'She's probably been prayed over in one of these "born-again" churches. That's what's been happening to one or two of my patients—or ex-patients, I should say.' And so Jenny's consultant had to admit that Jenny was a walking mystery to him—and a walking miracle to us. And with that miracle I realised that the prayer I'd received in the past for the ability to speak in tongues had to have been answered, so that what I'd thought was a natural ability to 'make up' a tongue must have been the real thing all the time!

I know that for all of us who want God to come first in our lives—as long as we're willing to obey him there's so much more in every way. So many more discoveries to make, and so much more dying to do, as we let him have his way in turning us from self-centred to Jesus-centred people. And so much more living to do too, as we become the neighbours he needs us to be at home, at work, at church, and in the communities he gives us to live in. We've many more neighbours to meet and help and be helped by in his life-transforming plan for us; some we'll like and some we initially won't, till his love in action—in our actions—takes over. And we've many more miracles to experience with the neighbours he's already given us, as we're ready for anything our praise and obediences can produce for them—however hopeless some of their situations might seem! (The ones we can't help he'll use our prayers to direct us to someone who can, and he'll do likewise for the ones the enemy sends to disrupt our lives, too. All we need is to keep on praising God for every special person he allows our way, knowing that in his eyes we're all special, whatever the world might say.)

Who needs neighbours? Every single one of us—whether we want them or not! So let's start loving each other his way, according to his instructions, without sentiment but with honest 'going the second mile' commitment. And the more we practise listening to his minute-by-minute instructions, the more we're going to know the beauty and brilliance of his totally personalised 'love your neighbour' plan. Personal to you, to me, and to every neighbour he ever sends our way!